Preface to the second edition

This second edition continues the main strength of the first edition, which is to have lessons based on texts written by professionals in their fields with PhDs. With these texts, students can be assured that they will learn important vocabulary and content used in the fields of engineering as practiced today.

The main changes in the second edition are the inclusions of new texts, namely those in biology, chemistry, gene science, solar power and artificial intelligence. Additionally, the English learning activities in each lesson have been streamlined, ensuring extensive practice in the four skills.

We are confident that students who use this book actively and with sustained effort will be able to substantially improve their knowledge and skills in English, and will make good progress towards the goal of English fluency.

National Institute of Technology, Tsuyama College
Eric Rambo
Kato Manabu

JN033380

Contents ・ もくじ

Preface to the first edition

本書で学習する皆さんへ

　本書は技術英語をこれから学ぼうと思っている学生諸君のために作成されました。技術職を目指す学生諸君のなかには、「どうも英語が苦手だ。」「自分は将来技術で飯を食っていくのだから英語なんて余り必要がない。」と考えている人が多いように見受けられます。しかし今後のグローバル社会を担う技術者となる諸君は、実践的な技術英語を身につけていることが非常に期待されているのです。会社では英語の技術論文や仕様書を読み、海外との英語によるメールや手紙のやり取りを行い、海外技術者との英語でのディスカッションなど、英語の基礎力なしではもはや社会では通用しません。

　このような背景のもと、英語が苦手、あるいは必要性を余り感じていない技術系学生諸君はもちろんのこと、技術英語の基礎をマスターしたいと考えている皆さんのために本書を作成しました。本書は津山高専における一般英語科の教員と専門学科の教員が連携して作成したもので、英文は企業経験や国際会議などを通じて技術英語に堪能な専門学科の教員が書き、一方注釈・文法・リスニング・ライティングなどは英語科の教員が担当しました。一般及び専門教員の連携により「実践的な活きた技術英語力」が効率よく身につくと思います。

　本書は「初級〜中級レベル」のテキストを目指して作成されています。今後はさらなる高度な技術英語のテキストを現在計画しています。本書を活用することにより、将来の技術者としての基礎英語力が修得されることを期待しております。

　なお本テキスト内容の校正には神戸高専・電気工学科教授の津吉彰氏の力をお借りしました。さらに原稿から出版までに対し、電気書院の田中建三郎氏、田中昇氏にいろいろとお世話になりました。これらの方々に感謝申し上げます。

津山高専・技術英語テキスト編集委員会

代表　　中岡尚美

副代表　伊藤國雄

執筆者　Eric Rambo
松田　修
古樋直己
寺元貴幸
細谷和範
久保川晴美
西尾公裕
加藤　学

改訂新版

技術英語

Second Edition
Technical English
A hands-on textbook for lower to intermediate level learners

実践的技術英語テキスト 初級〜中級レベル

Topics from:

Advanced Science・先進科学

Mechanical Systems・機械システム

Electrical and Electronic Systems・電気電子システム

Communication and Information Systems・情報システム

津山工業高等専門学校
技術英語テキスト改訂ワーキンググループ 編

電気書院

To Students:

With this book you will learn how to use basic technical English and improve your overall English ability. Especially, you will learn:	このテキストを使って、みなさんは基本的な技術英語の使い方を学び、英語力全般を上達させることができます。特に
▸ *4 skills (speaking, listening, reading, and writing)*	次の点を学べます。
▸ *Vocabulary*	○英語の４技能
▸ *Grammar*	○ボキャブラリー
▸ *Pronunciation*	○文法
With this book, you will do:	○発音
▪ *Individual work*	このテキストでは、次の活動をします。
▪ *Pair work*	○個人での学習
▪ *Self-evaluation (to check your progress)*	○ペアワーク
Your teachers will help you, but it is up to you to do the work. In particular:	○自己評価（自分の到達度をチェック）
1) You will need to study and practice (the vocabulary, the pronunciation, the grammar, etc.) over and over, until you are confident.	先生が手を貸してくれるかもしれませんが、やるかやらないかはあなたたち次第です。特に次の２つがポイントです。
2) You should familiarize yourself with the activities in this book, so that you can get the most out of them. Each lesson has the same activities.	1）ボキャブラリー、発音、文法などを繰り返し勉強し、演習すること。そうすれば自信がつきます。
Finally, technical English and the activities in this book may be a little difficult at first. But the rewards are great: you will be able to read English books, reports, and manuals, understand English technical presentations, get a higher TOEIC score, and more. So, if you make a good, sustained effort, you will make great progress.	2）このテキストで行ういろいろな活動に慣れてください。そうすれば、とても役に立ちます。各課は同じ活動をするように構成されています。
	このテキストの技術英語と活動は、最初は少し難しいかもしれません。けれども、大きく報われます。すなわち、英語の本、レポート、マニュアルを読めるようになるでしょう。また、英語のプレゼンテーションが理解できるようになります。そして TOEIC でも高得点がとれるでしょう。もっと良いことがあるかもしれません。だから、きちんと継続して努力すれば、英語が上達するでしょう。

Lesson 1: Advanced science *and* Mechanical engineering

▸ Listen to the instructor pronounce the words, and repeat. Check your pronunciation.

▸ Memorize the spelling and meaning.

mechanical	機械の	physics	物理学	to design	設計する
electrical	電気の	to develop	発展する	control	制御
chemical	化学	interdisciplinary	学際的な	engineering	工学
engineering	工学	field	分野	transmission	変速機
century	世紀	precise	精密な	brakes	ブレーキ
discipline	領域	measurement	測定、計測	body	本体、胴体
to arise	起こる	technical	工学の	tough	頑丈な
genetic	遺伝学の	material	材料	flight	飛行
biology	生物学	machine	機械		

2. Reading

▸ Read and study the text. Use the *Text notes* on p. 2.

Advanced science *and* Mechanical engineering

1 The world of engineering consists of many branches and includes Mechanical, Electrical, Computer, Chemical engineering, etc. However, starting towards the end of the 20th century, new disciplines arose, such as *genetic engineering*.

With this rise, Advanced science has become an even more important part of engineering.
5 Advanced science includes mathematics, biology, chemistry, and physics. It has developed into many new interdisciplinary fields, as mentioned above. Therefore, skills in Advanced science, such as precise measurement, are important for all engineering and technical fields.

Mechanical engineering is the study of machines and materials. It is one of the oldest engineering fields. All machines are designed based on
10 mechanical engineering. For example, a car has an engine or motor, a transmission, brakes, and a body, all of which are designed based on mechanical engineering.

An important part of Mechanical engineering is control engineering. With control engineering, we can control one machine with another machine.
15 Let's take a heavy lift launch vehicle as an example. The rocket engine, the tough body, and the computer systems work together to control the flight. Thus it can be said that mechanical and control engineering work together, like a pair of wheels.

3. Text notes

line 2: towards the end of the 20th century 「20 世紀末にかけて」

I.5: It has developed into ～ 「～へと発展した」

I.6: interdisciplinary fields 「学際的領域」 as mentioned above 「前述したように」

I.8: one of the oldest engineering fields 「最も古い工学分野の１つ」

I.9: based on mechanical engineering 「機械工学に基づいて」

I.13: control engineering 「制御工学」

I.15: take ～ as an example 「～を例にする」「～を例として挙げる」

I.15: a heavy lift launch vehicle 「重量物打ち上げロケット」

I.17: Thus it can be said that ～ 「したがって、～と言える」

I.17: a pair of wheels 「1 組の車輪」「両輪」

4. Reading comprehension (読解) and Reading aloud (音読)

1. By yourself, or with a partner, answer these questions. Then check with the instructor.

   ▶ What are the main points of: *the first paragraph*? *the second*? *the third*? *the fourth*?

   I understand each paragraph: ☐ Yes ☐ Not yet (→ *check the translation on p. 73*)

2. Now, with a partner, read the text aloud (one paragraph at a time). Read smoothly, with good pronunciation.

   ▶ How was your reading and pronunciation? ☐ Good ☐ Needs more practice

5. Discussion

▶ Write your answers. Then check the instructor's answers.

▶ Ask your partner the questions. If you like, ask "follow-up" questions.

1. What does Advanced science include? Why is it important?	
2. What are some examples of interdisciplinary fields?	
3. What is mechanical engineering? Why is it important?	
4. A heavy lift launch vehicle a good example of mechanical and control engineering. Why?	

Self evaluation → I spoke 100% in English: ☐ Yes ☐ No

6. Dictation

▶ Write what your instructor says. With a red pen, check.

----

7. Exercises

A. ▶Think of the correct words, and write them. Check with a red pen.

1. The world of engineering consists of _____ and includes…

2. However, starting _____ of the 20th century, new…

3. Mechanical engineering is the study of _____.

4. For _____ , a car has an engine or motor, a _____ ,…

5. Thus it _____ that mechanical and control engineering work together,…

B. ▶ Circle the correct answer. Check, and think of the reason.

1. With this rise, Advanced science has (became / become) an even more important part of…

2. It has (developing / developed) into many interdisciplinary fields, as mentioned above.

3. Therefore, skills (in / to) Advanced science are important for all engineering fields.

4. With control engineering, we can control one machine (to / with) another machine.

5. Let's (taking / take) a heavy lift launch vehicle as an example.

C. ▶ Write the correct word form (n = noun 名詞　v = verb 動詞 adj = adjective 形容詞 etc.)
    ▶ Think of grammatically correct sentences for each word.

biology (n)　　　→　(adj)_____

to develop (v)　　→　(n)_____

3

8. Translation

▶ Translate the sentences into English. Check and correct your work (→ see p. 80).

1. 科学と工学は、相互に関連した学問領域です。

2. 科学と工学、いずれにおいても正確な計測が重要です。

3. 僕の車は、最新モデルの一つで、環境にとてもやさしく設計されている。

4. 先生は、外燃熱機関を説明するためによくロケットエンジンを例として取り上げる。

9. Writing

1. Write a summary of the text on p. 1. (*This text is about… It starts with… It says that… For example,… Then it…*). Include your *feelings* and *ideas* about the topic.

- - *OR* - -

2. Write an essay following your instructor's directions.

(→you can also type and improve your essay, and use it for a spoken presentation)

10. Extended reading and Review

▶ Search the Internet for related readings. Choose one and read. (If you like, use GOOGLE TRANSLATE to help you understand.) What article did you choose? What is it about?

▶ Review the *vocabulary*, *reading* and *exercises* in this lesson. What words, sentences, or ideas are difficult? Why?

4

Lesson 2: Electrical engineering *and* Information engineering

1. Vocabulary

▶ Listen and repeat. Memorize.

household	家庭用の	equipment	装置	hardware	ハードウェア
goods	商品	electronic	電子	word processor	ワードプロセッサ
to function	機能する	function	機能	document	書類
washing machine	洗濯機	electrical	電気	furthermore	さらに、その上
to supply	供給する	personal computer	パソコン	seamlessly	シームレスに
battery	電池	to run	作動させる	social media	ソーシャルメディア
adaptor	アダプター	software	ソフトウェア		

2. Reading

▶ Read and study the text.

Electrical engineering *and* Information engineering

1   Electrical engineering is the study of electricity and the design of electrical machines. All household electrical goods use electricity in order to function. For example, televisions, washing machines, and computers all use electricity. The electricity can be supplied to the machine by a battery, a power supply adaptor, or other power supply equipment. The electronic functions of all of 5   these machines have been designed by electrical engineers.

     Information engineering is the study of computer hardware and software, and how these are used in society. A good example is the personal computer (PC). The personal computer runs software like email and word processors that we use to communicate and make documents. Furthermore, the computer is designed 10 to function seamlessly with the Internet, so that we can easily listen to music, read news, make purchases, study, and, if we wish, engage in social media. All of these computer functions have been designed by computer engineers.

     We will look more closely at how this hardware and software works in Lesson 3.

I 2: in order to ～　「～するために」という目的の意味を表す。(= so as to ~)

I.3: can be supplied　「供給されることができる」「補充されることができる」

I.8: like ～　「～のような」「～と同様に」「たとえば～のような」

I.8: email and word processors that we use
　　「私たちが使っている『メール』やワードプロセッサ」

I.9: designed to function seamlessly with ～「～とシームレスに機能するように設計されている」

I.13: more closely　「もっと詳細に」「もっと詳しく」

I.13: We will look more closely at how this hardware and software works
　　「どのようにこのハードウェアとソフトウェアが動いているのか、もっと詳細に見ていきましょう。」

1. By yourself, or with a partner, answer these questions. Then check with the instructor.

▸ What are the main points of: *the first paragraph*? *the second*? *the third*?

I understand each paragraph: ☐ Yes ☐ Not yet

2. Now, with a partner, read the text aloud. Read smoothly, with good pronunciation.

▸ How was your reading and pronunciation? ☐ Good ☐ Needs more practice

▸ Write, then ask. If you like, ask "follow-up" questions.

1. What is electrical engineering? Why is it important?	
2. What are your favorite household electrical goods? Why?	
3. What is information engineering? Why is it important?	
4. What kind of software can PCs run? To do what?	
5. What Internet sites do you use regularly? Why?	

Self evaluation → 　　I spoke 100% in English: ☐ Yes ☐ No

6. Dictation

▶ Write what your instructor says. With a red pen, check your work.

----

7. Exercises

A. ▶ Think, write. Check with a red pen.

1. All household electrical goods use electricity _____ function.

2. The electricity can _____ to the machine by a battery, a...

3. The electronic functions of all of _____ have been designed by...

4. The personal computer runs _____ email and word processors...

5. Furthermore, the computer _____ function seamlessly with the Internet,...

B. ▶ Circle the correct answer. Check, and think of the reason.

1. The electronic functions of all of these machines (have / have been) designed by...

2. The personal computer (runs / is running) software like email and web processors that...

3. Furthermore, the computer is designed to function (seemingly / seamlessly) with the Internet,...

4. All of these computer (functions / function) have been designed by computer engineers.

5. We will look more (close / closely) at how this hardware and software works in Lesson 3.

C. ▶ Write the correct word form, and think of correct sentences.

electrical (adj) → _(n)_ _____ → _(adj)_ _____

to supply (v) → _(n) a_ _____

equipment (n) → _(v) to_ _____

7

8. Translation

1. 私たちはエンジニアになるために電気電子工学を学ぶ。

2. 私は外国で働くために英語をマスターしたい。

3. インターネットは私たちの生活の一部になりました。

4. 情報工学の発展は、私達の生活に何をもたらしましたか？

9. Writing

1. Write a summary of the text on p. 5. Include your feelings and ideas about the topic.
- - OR - -
2. Write an essay following your instructor's directions.

10. Extended reading and Review

▶ Search the Internet for related readings. What article did you choose? What is it about?

▶ Review this lesson. What *words*, *sentences*, or *ideas* are difficult? Why?

Lesson 3: The personal computer

1. Vocabulary

▶ Listen and repeat. Memorize.

individual	個人	part	部分、部品	complicated	複雑な
type	型、タイプ	central processing unit	中央処理装置	performance	性能
standard	標準の	circuit	回路	however	しかしながら
lap	ひざ	to execute	〜を実行する	portable	持ち運びできる
compact	無駄なスペースのない	program	プログラム	lithium	リチウム
recently	最近	command	コマンド	ion	イオン
tablet	タブレット	to allow	〜を許す、〜に…させる	density	密度
to compose	〜を構成する				

2. Reading

▶ Read and study the text.

The personal computer

1   A computer that is designed to be used by an individual is called a personal computer, or PC. There are several types of PCs. First is the standard desk-top computer. Next is the smaller and more compact lap-top. In Japan, a lap-top PC is called a *notebook* computer. Third is the *tablet* computer, which has a touch screen. The number of tablet computers sold has recently increased.

5   A PC is composed of many parts. Today, we will talk about the CPU, or the *central processing unit*. The CPU is the most important part of a computer. The CPU is the electronic circuits that execute a computer program. For example, the CPU executes the commands that allow you to use Microsoft Word® and to read internet pages. The CPU is a very complicated electric circuit. The performance of the CPU greatly
10   affects the performance of the PC. If the CPU is fast, then the computer will be fast.

     However, a high-performance CPU consumes a lot of electric power. Therefore, the performance of the battery is important for a portable PC. Recently, a light "lithium ion" battery has been used because the electric power density of this type of battery is high.

     Can you explain what a CPU does? Do you know how a "lithium ion" battery stores electricity?

3. Text notes

l.1: be designed to 動詞の原形 「～するように設計されている」

The IC is designed to run from 1.5V to 4.8V.

(その IC は 1.5V から 4.8V で動作するように設計されている。)

l.4: the number of ～ 「～の数」

The number of the students is increasing.

(学生の人数は増加している。)

l.5: be composed of ～ 「～でできている」

ICs are composed of many transistors and other electronic components.

(IC は多くのトランジスタや他の電子部品でできている。)

l.8: allow A to 動詞の原形 「A が～するのを許可(可能に)する」

The software allows us to use pdf files on this PC.

(そのソフトはこの PC で pdf ファイルを使えるようにしてくれる。)

l.10: affect 「～に影響する」

l.12: has been used 「使われてきている」 ＜受身の現在完了形＞

l.14: store 「～を蓄える」

4. Reading comprehension and Reading aloud

1. By yourself, or with a partner, answer these questions. Then check with the instructor.

   ▶ What are the main points of *the first paragraph*? *the second*? *the third*? *the fourth*?

   I understand each paragraph: ☐ Yes ☐ Not yet

2. Now, with a partner, read the text aloud. Read smoothly, with good pronunciation.

   ▶ How was your reading and pronunciation? ☐ Good ☐ Needs more practice

5. Discussion

▶ Write, then ask. If you like, ask "follow-up" questions.

1. What are the different types of PCs?	
2. What is a CPU? What does it do?	
3. What does a CPU allow us to do?	
4. Why does a CPU consume a lot of power?	

Self evaluation → I spoke 100% in English: ☐ Yes ☐ No

6. Dictation

▸ Write what your instructor says. With a red pen, check.

----

7. Exercises

A. ▸ Think, write. Check with a red pen.

1. A computer that is _____ to be used by an individual is _____ a PC.

2. The number of tablet computers sold has _____.

3. Today, we will talk about the CPU, or the _____.

4. The CPU is the electronic circuits _____ a computer program.

5. Do you know _____ a "lithium ion" battery _____ electricity?

B. ▸ Circle the correct answer. Check, and think of the reason.

1. There are several (type / types) of PCs.

2. Third is the tablet computer, which has a (touch / touching) screen.

3. The CPU is (a / the) most important part of a computer.

4. However, a high-performance CPU consumes (many / a lot of) electric power.

5. Can you explain (that / what) a CPU does?

C. ▸ Write the correct word form, and think of correct sentences.

an individual
(n)   →   (adv) _____

a program
(n)   →   (n) _____ → (v) _____
                    (hint: it is a gerund)

8. Translation

1. 先月、その会社はいくつかの新しいコンピューターを発売した。 ＊発売する　release

2. その一つは、ラップトップタイプで、初心者が使えるように設計されている。

3. それは、最小限の部品でできているが、レポート作成や e-mail 送信には十分な能力を有する。
＊最小限の　minimum

4. それはその会社のすべてのコンピューターの中でもっとも軽く、もっとも安い。

9. Writing

1. Write a summary of the text on p. 9. Include your feelings and ideas about the topic.

- - OR - -

2. Write an essay following your instructor's directions.

10. Extended reading and Review

▶ Search the Internet for related readings. What article did you choose? What is it about?

▶ Review this lesson. What *words*, *sentences*, or *ideas* are difficult? Why?

Lesson 4: Opto-electronic devices

1. Vocabulary

▶ Listen and repeat. Memorize.

diode	ダイオード	sensor	センサ	traffic	交通
semiconductor	半導体	to arrange	配列する	bulletin board	掲示板
material	素材、材料	cellular phone	携帯電話	special	特別な
to convert	変換する	linear	直線の	laser	レーザ
signal	信号	array	配列	to focus	集光する
input	入力	energy	エネルギー	printer	プリンタ
image	画像	to emit	放射する		

2. Reading

▶ Read and study the text.

Opto-electronic devices

1   Do you know how a digital camera works? It uses a diode. A diode is made with a semiconducting material, like silicon. Today, we will talk about three types of diodes.

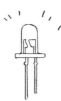

The first type is a photodiode (Figure 1). It converts light into an electric
5   signal. For example, the photodiodes in a digital camera convert the light of the picture image into an electric signal. This signal is the electrical input for the *image sensors**. Image sensors can be arranged in two ways. One is called a *linear array sensor*, and is used in fax machines. The other is called an *area array sensor*. It is used in digital cameras,
10   video camcorders, and cellular phones.

Figure 1

The second type of diode converts electric energy into light. It is called a light-emitting diode, or LED (Figure 2). LEDs are used in traffic lights, electric bulletin boards, and other electric machines. Can you think of some other machines that use LEDs?

15   Finally, there is the "laser diode". The light from the laser is very strong

Figure 2

and focused. The laser diode is used for compact disc players, laser printers and other machines.

All of these diodes are called opto-electronic devices. Do you know why? (Hint: opto = optical).

* image sensors are called "charge coupled devices" (CCD), and "complementary metal oxide semiconductors" (CMOS)

13

3. Text notes

l.1: be made with ～　「～でできている」
　　An IC is made with silicon.（ICはシリコンでできている。）
l.4: the first type　「最初のタイプ」「前者」
l.4: convert A into B　「AをBに変換する」
　　The software converts wav into MP3.
　　（このソフトはwavファイルをMP3ファイルへ変換してくれる。）
l.8: One is called A. The other is called B.「Aと呼ばれるものもあれば，Bと呼ばれるものもある。」
l.8: be used in ～　「～に使われている」
　　Many transistors are used in the equipment.
　　（多くのトランジスタがその機器に使われている。）
l.16: be used for ～「～に使われている」　be used in と同様

4. Reading comprehension and Reading aloud

1. By yourself, or with a partner, answer these questions. Then check with the instructor.

▶ What are the main points of: *the first paragraph*? *the second*? *the third*? *the fourth*? *the fifth*?

I understand each paragraph:　☐ Yes　　☐ Not yet

2. Now, with a partner, read the text aloud. Read smoothly, with good pronunciation.

▶ How was your reading and pronunciation?　☐ Good　　☐ Needs more practice

5. Discussion

▶ Write, then ask. If you like, ask "follow-up" questions.

1. What are the three types of diodes? Can you spell those words?	
2. What does a photodiode do? How? What machines use them?	
3. What does a light-emitting diode do? What machines use them?	
4. How about a laser diode? What machines use them?	

Self evaluation →　　　　I spoke 100% in English:　☐ Yes　　☐ No

14

▸ Write what your instructor says. With a red pen, check.

----

7. Exercises

A. ▸ Think, write. Check with a red pen.

1. A diode is _____ a semiconducting _____ , like silicon.

2. The first type is a photodiode. It converts light _____ signal.

3. It _____ in digital cameras, video camcorders, and cellular phones.

4. Can you think of _____ that use LEDs?

5. All of these diodes are called opto-electronic _____. Do _____ know why?

B. ▸ Circle the correct answer. Check, and think of the reason.

1. A diode is made with (a / the) semiconducting material, like silicon.

2. Today, we will (talking / talk) about three types of diodes.

3. Image sensors can be arranged (through / in) two ways.

4. LEDs are used in traffic lights, electric bulletin boards, and (another / other) electric machines.

5. The light (by / from) the laser is very strong and (focus / focused).

C. ▸ Write the correct word form, and think of correct sentences.

to arrange (v)   →   (n) an _____

to emit (v)   →   (n) an _____

printer (n)   →   (v) _____

15

8. Translation

1. 電流には2つの種類がある。1つは直流と呼ばれ、もう1つは交流と呼ばれている。

2. 家庭での電化製品には、交流が使われている。

3. このアダプターは、交流を直流に変換してくれる。

4. 最近の信号機にはLEDが使用され、白熱球との置き換えが進んでいる。

9. Writing

1. Write a summary of the text on p. 13. Include your feelings and ideas about the topic.

- - OR - -

2. Write an essay following your instructor's directions.

----

10. Extended reading and Review

▶ Search the Internet for related readings. What article did you choose? What is it about?

▶ Review this lesson. What *words*, *sentences*, or *ideas* are difficult? Why?

Lesson 5:   Reproduction: Switching of reproductive modes in planarians

▸ Listen and repeat. Memorize.

reproduction	生殖	to involve	必要	to regenerate	再生させること
broadly	広く	diversity	多様性	to mate	交尾すること
sexual	有性の	mate	交尾相手	to lay	産むこと
asexual	無性の	freshwater	淡水性の	cocoon	卵殻
individual	個体	mode	様式	to fertilize	受精すること
gene	遺伝子	fragment	断片	to prosper	繁栄すること
thus	このように				

▸ Read and study the text.

Reproduction: Switching of reproductive modes in planarians

1 Reproduction is broadly divided into sexual and asexual reproduction. "Reproduction" is defined as the increase of similar individuals, and "sex" is defined as the mixing of genes. Sexual reproduction thus involves the mixing of genes to increase the number of individuals. It can produce diversity, but the reproductive cost is high. Asexual reproduction does not involve the mixing of genes, and
5 has a low reproductive cost because there is no need to find a mate. However, it is difficult to produce diversity.

Many animals reproduce both asexually and sexually. They can switch between two reproductive modes depending on
10 environmental conditions. For example, some freshwater planarians switch reproductive modes (Fig. 1)[1]. In asexual reproduction, planarians divide their bodies into two pieces, and the fragments regenerate the lost parts. In
15 sexual reproduction, hermaphroditic planarians mate and lay cocoons containing fertilized eggs.

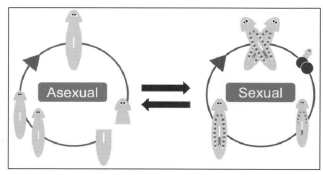

Fig.1 Switching of Reproductive Modes

The freshwater planarian *Dugesia japonica* reproduce asexually in the summer and sexually in the winter[2]. It is thought that they have prospered by using two reproductive modes depending on the
20 season.

1) Kobayashi et al., 1999. Zool. Sci.
2) Maezawa et al., 2018. Bull. of NIT, Tsuyama Col.

17

l.1: is defined as ～　「～と定義される」

l.4: reproductive cost　「生殖コスト 」

l.9: depending on ～　「～に依存する」

l.10: environmental conditions　「環境条件」

l.11: freshwater planarians「淡水性プラナリア」

l.15: hermaphroditic planarians　「雌雄同体のプラナリア」

l.16: mate and lay cocoons　「交尾して卵殻を産む」

l.16: fertilized eggs　「受精卵」

l.19: It is thought that ～　「～と考えられる」

l.19: they have prospered　「それらは繁栄してきた」

4. Reading comprehension and Reading aloud

1. By yourself, or with a partner, answer these questions. Then check with the instructor.

▸ What are the main points of:　*the first paragraph*?　*the second*?　*the third*?

I understand each paragraph:　☐ Yes　☐ Not yet

2. Now, with a partner, read the text aloud. Read smoothly, with good pronunciation.

▸ How was your reading and pronunciation?　☐ Good　☐ Needs more practice

5. Discussion

▸ Write, then ask. If you like, ask "follow-up" questions.

1. In the first paragraph, what does "reproductive cost" mean? Explain.	
2. Also in the first paragraph, what does "diversity" mean? Explain and give examples.	
3. How do planarians reproduce asexually? Sexually?	
4. In the last paragraph what does "have prospered" mean? Explain.	

Self evaluation →　　I spoke 100% in English:　☐ Yes　　☐ No

6. Dictation

▶ Write what your instructor says. With a red pen, check.

----

7. Exercises

A. ▶ Think, write. Check with a red pen.

1. "Reproduction" is _____ the increase of _____ individuals,…

2. It can produce _____ , but the reproductive _____ is high.

3. Many animals reproduce both asexually and _____.

4. In asexual reproduction, planarians divide _____ two pieces, and the…

5. It is thought that they _____ by using two reproductive modes…

B. ▶ Circle the correct answer. Check, and think of the reason.

1. Asexual reproduction has (the / a) low reproductive cost because there is no need to find a mate.

2. However, it is difficult to (producing / produce) diversity.

3. They can switch between two reproductive modes (depending / depended) on...

4. In asexual reproduction, planarians divide (them / their) bodies into two pieces, and…

5. In sexual reproduction, hermaphroditic planarians (mate / to mate) and lay cocoons.

C. ▶ Write the correct word form, and think of correct sentences.

reproduction (n) → (v) _____

diversity (n) → (v) _____

to fertilize (v) → (n) _____

19

8. Translation

1. 多くの動物は無性的および有性的に生殖を行うことができます。

2. 無性生殖は多様性を生み出すことができません。

3. 淡水性プラナリアの中には生殖様式を転換させないグループもいます。

4. 淡水性プラナリアは夏と冬の間に無性生殖から有性生殖へ転換させます。

9. Writing

1. Write a summary of the text on p. 17. Include your feelings and ideas about the topic.

- - OR - -

2. Write an essay following your instructor's directions.

10. Extended reading and Review

▶ Search the Internet for related readings. What article did you choose? What is it about?

▶ Review this lesson. What *words*, *sentences*, or *ideas* are difficult? Why?

Lesson 6:   Ohm's law

1. Vocabulary

▸ Listen and repeat. Memorize.

fundamental	基本の	resistance	抵抗	value	値
law	法則	physicist	物理学者	condition	状態、条件
basic	基本的な	to discover	発見する	constant	一定の
current	電流	proportional	～に比例している	reciprocal	逆の
to represent	～を表す	equation	方程式	conductance	コンダクタンス
voltage	電圧				

2. Reading

▸ Read and study the text.

Ohm's law

1   In this lesson we will learn about the fundamental law of the electric circuit. This law is called Ohm's law. It is used for all electrical circuits.

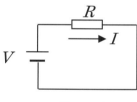

Figure 1

Look at Figure 1. It is a basic electric circuit. The electric current is represented by *I*, voltage by *V*, and resistance by *R*.* The German
5   physicist Georg Simon Ohm (1789 - 1854) discovered that electric current is proportional to the voltage. This discovery is now called Ohm's law. This law is given in the following equation,

$$I = \frac{V}{R}$$

We call *R electric resistance*, or just *resistance*. When *R* is a large value, *I* becomes a small value under the condition that *V* is constant. Under the same condition, *I* becomes a large value when *R*
10   is small. For example, in a circuit with a small resistance, a large amount of electrical current can flow.

On the other hand, the reciprocal number *G=1/R* is called *conductance***. In this case, Ohm's law is represented by the following equation, *I = GV.*   For example, if the conductance is high, then more electrical current can flow.

15   Now, can you explain Ohm's law in English? Remember, you need to explain *current*, *voltage*, *resistance*, and *conductance*.

* Resistance is measured in ohms "Ω", electric current in amperes "A", and voltage in volts "V".
** Conductance is measured in Siemens "S".

21

3. Text notes

l.1: learn about ～ 「～について学ぶ」
l.2: be called ～ 「～と呼ばれている」
    The component is called an oscillation device.（その部品は，発振素子と呼ばれている。）
l.2: be used for ～ 「～に使われる」
l.2: electric(al) circuit 「電気回路」
l.4: be represented by ～ 「～と表される」
l.6: be proportional to ～ 「～に比例している」
    日本語の「プロポーションがよい・悪い」は，身体の各部位の比率のことを言っている。
l.6: discovery 「発見」（discover の名詞形）
l.7: be given in ～ 「～に与えられている」 following 「下記の，つぎの」

4. Reading comprehension and Reading aloud

1. By yourself, or with a partner, answer these questions. Then check with the instructor.

  ▶ What are the main points of: *the <u>first</u> <u>paragraph</u>? the <u>second</u>? the <u>third</u>? the <u>fourth</u>? the <u>fifth</u>?*

      I understand each paragraph: ☐ Yes   ☐ Not yet

2. Now, with a partner, read the text aloud. Read smoothly, with good pronunciation.

  ▶ How was your reading and pronunciation?   ☐ Good   ☐ Needs more practice

5. Discussion

▶ Write, then ask. If you like, ask "follow-up" questions.

1. Who was Georg Simon Ohm? Do you admire him? Why?	
2. What is Ohm's law? Explain.	
3. What happens when *R* is increased? Decreased?	
4. What is conductance? Explain.	

Self evaluation →   I spoke 100% in English: ☐ Yes   ☐ No

6. Dictation

▸ Write what your instructor says. With a red pen, check.

----

7. Exercises

A. ▸ Think, write. Check with a red pen.

1. In this lesson we will learn about the _____ law of the electric circuit.

2. The electric current is represented by I, _____ by V, and _____ by R.

3. When R is a large value, I becomes a small value under the condition that V is _____.

4. In a circuit with a small resistance, a _____ amount of electrical current can flow

5. On the other hand, the _____ number $G=1/R$ is called _____.

B. ▸ Circle the correct answer. Check, and think of the reason.

1. This law is called Ohm's law. It is used (for / by) all electrical circuits.

2. When R is (the / a) large value, I becomes (the / a) small value under the condition that…

3. …discovered that electric current is proportional to (the /a) voltage.

4. Under the same condition, I (becomes / is becoming) a large value when R is small.

5. For example, if the conductance is high, (when / then) more electrical current can flow.

C. ▸ Write the correct word form, and think of correct sentences.

basic (adj) → (adv) _____

a physicist (n) → (n) _____

to discover (v) → (n) a _____

23

8. Translation

1. オームの法則は、電気工学において基礎的な知識です。

2. この電気回路に流れる電流は、オームの法則を用いて計算しました。

3. 電気製品には機能を向上させるために、レアメタルが使用されている.

4. その一方で、多くのレアメタルが、無意識に捨てられている。　　＊無意識に　unconsciously
　　　　　　　　　　　　　　　　　　　　　　　　　　　　　　　　　＊捨てる　dump

9. Writing

1. Write a summary of the text on p. 21, including your feelings and ideas.

- - OR - -

2. Write an essay following your instructor's directions.

----

10. Extended reading and Review

▶ Search the Internet for related readings. What article did you choose? What is it about?

▶ Review this lesson. What *words*, *sentences*, or *ideas* are difficult? Why?

Lesson 7:   Solar power generation with photovoltaic (PV) cells

1. Vocabulary

▸ Listen and repeat. Memorize.

fuel	燃料	to concentrate	（光を）集める	grid	（電力）系統
photovoltaic	太陽光発電の	to focus	〜を集める	widespread	広い
renewable	再生可能な	irradiance	日射光	adoption	採用
term	用語	accurately	正確に	crucial	重要
to describe	〜を表す	to track	〜を追尾する	emissions	排出
crystalline	結晶	to maintain	〜を合わせる	sector	分野
silicon	シリコン（Si）	complexity	複雑さ	to enhance	〜を強化する
module	モジュール	to mount	〜を搭載する	security	安全保障

2. Reading

▸ Read and study the text.

Solar power generation with photovoltaic (PV) cells

1   "Renewable energy" is a term used to describe generating electricity from natural sources that are not fossil fuels or nuclear power. Today, we will take a close look at getting power from the sun, with photovoltaic cells.
5   This is called "solar power generation".

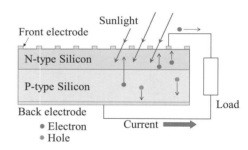

Fig. 1. Diagram of a PV cell.

A photovoltaic (PV) cell converts sunlight into electrical energy. To do this, it uses semiconductor materials, such as crystalline silicon (Fig. 1). Can you explain this figure?

A PV *module* includes multiple PV cells. There are 2 types
10 of PV modules. The first is called a **concentrator**. Concentrator modules (Fig. 2) use lenses to focus solar irradiance on the PV cells. However, they need to accurately track the sun in order to maintain focus, which adds cost and complexity. The second type is called a
15 **flat plate** module (Fig. 3), which can be mounted at fixed angles. These are commonly used in solar farms.

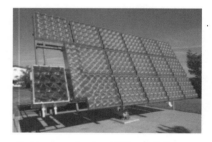

Fig. 2. Concentrator PV modules mounted on a solar tracking system (NIT, Tsuyama College).

PV modules generate direct current (DC) power, which cannot be directly used in most homes, or transmitted to the power grid. Therefore, the DC power needs to be
20 converted into alternating current (AC) power.

The widespread adoption of PV power generation is crucial not only for reducing carbon emissions in the energy sector, but also for enhancing national energy security. In the future, PV power generation is expected to
25 play an even more critical role in our society.

Fig 3. Flat plate modules comprising a PV array (NIT, Tsuyama College).

3. Text notes

Title: photovoltaic cells 「太陽電池」

l.1: a term used to describe ～ 「～を説明するために使われる用語」

l.2: generating electricity「発電」 fossil fuels or nuclear power 「化石燃料または原子力」

l.11: use lenses to focus solar irradiance on ～ 「～にレンズを使って日射を集める」

l.13: in order to maintain focus 「焦点を合わせるために」

l.15: at fixed angles 「一定の角度」

l.23: enhancing national energy security 「国際エネルギー安全保障の強化」

l.25: even more critical role in ～ 「～にさらに重要な役割を果たす」

4. Reading comprehension and Reading aloud

1. By yourself, or with a partner, answer these questions. Then check with the instructor.

▶ What are the main points of: *the first paragraph*? *the second*? *the third*? *the fourth*? *the fifth*?

I understand each paragraph:　☐ Yes　　☐ Not yet

2. Now, with a partner, read the text aloud. Read smoothly, with good pronunciation.

▶ How was your reading and pronunciation?　☐ Good　　☐ Needs more practice

5. Discussion

▶ Write, then ask. If you like, ask "follow-up" questions.

1. What does "solar power generation" mean?	
2. What does a PV cell do? How? Explain Fig. 1.	
3. What are the two types of PV modules? What are the differences?	
4. What kind of power do PV modules generate? What needs to be done with it?	
5. Why is PV power generation crucial for "national energy security"?	

Self evaluation →　　　　I spoke 100% in English:　☐ Yes　　☐ No

6. Dictation

▶ Write what your instructor says. With a red pen, check.

----

7. Exercises

A.　▶ Think, write. Check with a red pen.

1. "Renewable energy" is a term used to _____ generating electricity from…

2. Today, we will take _____ at getting power from the sun,…

3. Concentrator modules use lenses _____ solar irradiance on the PV cells.

4. However, they need to _____ track the sun in order to maintain focus.

5. PV modules generate DC power, which cannot be _____ in most homes...

B.　▶ Circle the correct answer. Check, and think of the reason.

1. Today, we will take a close look at getting power (by / from) the sun.

2. This is (called / calling) "solar power generation".

3. This adds cost and (complexion / complexity).

4. The widespread adoption (to / of) PV power generation is crucial not only for reducing...

5. In the future, PV power generation is (expected / expecting) to play an even more crucial role.

C.　▶ Write the correct word form, and think of correct sentences.

renewable (adj)	→ (v) _____	complexity (n) →	(adj) _____
to describe (v)	→ (n) a _____	security (n) →	(adj) _____
accurately (adv)	→ (adj) _____		

27

8. Translation

1. 太陽光発電は、発電時に化石燃料を消費しない。

2. 集光式モジュールは、太陽電池、レンズ、および太陽追尾装置で構成される。

3. 太陽光発電の導入量が増加した理由のひとつは、そのコストの低下である。

4. 太陽光発電の導入は、地球温暖化を防ぐ有効な方法である。

9. Writing

1. Write a summary of the text on p. 25. Include your feelings and ideas about the topic.

- - OR - -

2. Write an essay following your instructor's directions.

----

10. Extended reading and Review

▶ Search the Internet for related readings. What article did you choose? What is it about?

▶ Review this lesson. What *words*, *sentences*, or *ideas* are difficult? Why?

Lesson 8:   Genome editing: A mouse with GFP

1. Vocabulary

▶ Listen and repeat. Memorize.

genome	ゲノム	blueprint	設計図	precise	正確な
biotechnology	バイオテクノロジー	resource	資源	process	過程、方法
organism	生物	to synthesize	合成すること	modification	改変
species	種	fluorescent	蛍光	to enable	可能にすること
molecule	分子	to absorb	を吸収する	to employ	利用すること
to inherit	受け継ぐこと	ultraviolet	紫外線	embryo	胚
protein	タンパク質	fusion	融合	ethical	倫理上の
sequence	配列	to derive	由来すること	innovation	革新、発明
gene	遺伝子	to recombine	組み替えること		

2. Reading

▶ Read and study the text.

Genome editing: A mouse with GFP

1   Recently, genome-based biotechnology has been developing rapidly. The "genome" is the total genetic information of organisms. Each species has its own specific genome. The main molecule of a genome is Deoxyribonucleic acid (DNA). In all organisms, DNA is inherited by children from their parents.

Proteins are important molecules in all life phenomena. DNA sequences called "genes" in the genome
5 act as blueprints of proteins. This means that **genes** are the resources for synthesizing proteins. For example, in the genome of a jellyfish, there is a gene to produce Green Fluorescent Protein (GFP)[1]. GFP emits green fluorescence when it absorbs ultraviolet light.

Today, GFP is used in many life sciences. For instance, we can make a "fusion protein" of a mouse protein and GFP. To do this, a
10 GFP gene derived from the jellyfish is put (or "recombined") in a precise location in a mouse genome. Please see Fig. 1. Can you explain this figure? When the process is completed, we can see the green fluorescence in living mouse cells *in vitro*, or trace the behavior of cells *in vivo*.

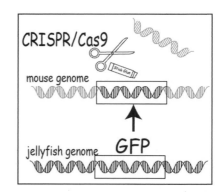

15 This is called the CRISPR/Cas9 "genome modification" method[2]. CRISPR/Cas9 has enabled us to perform genome modification quickly and accurately, at low-cost.

Fig. 1. A gene editing technique

Nowadays, genome modification based on CRISPR/Cas9 is employed in many research projects using various species. It is an important technological advancement. However, there are dangers. For
20 example, there was a report of CRISPR/Cas9 used in human embryos. This clearly indicates the ethical risks of this biotechnology. We have to never forget that any technical innovation is potentially a double-edged sword.

1) Shimomura et al., 1962. J. Cell Comp. Physiol.
2) Jinek et al., 2012. Science.

3. Text notes

l.1: developing rapidly 「急速に発展している」

l.1: total genetic information of ～ 「～の全遺伝情報」

l.3: Deoxyribonucleic acid (DNA) 「デオキシリボ核酸」

l.4: all life phenomena 「全ての生命現象」

l.7: emits green fluorescence 「緑色蛍光を発する」

l.13: *in vitro* 「試験管内（培養系）の（で）」（ラテン語はイタリックで示します）

l.13: trace the behavior of ～ 「～のふるまいをたどる」

l.14: *in vivo* 「体内の（で）」

l.20: this clearly indicates ～ 「これは明らかに～を示している」

l.21: potentially a double-edged sword 「潜在的に諸刃の剣」

4. Reading comprehension and Reading aloud

1. By yourself, or with a partner, answer these questions. Then check with the instructor.

▸ What are the main points of: *the first paragraph*? *the second*? *the third*? *the fourth*? *the fifth*?

I understand each paragraph: ☐ Yes ☐ Not yet

2. Now, with a partner, read the text aloud. Read smoothly, with good pronunciation.

▸ How was your reading and pronunciation? ☐ Good ☐ Needs more practice

5. Discussion

▸ Write, then ask. If you like, ask "follow-up" questions.

1.	What is a genome? Explain.	
2.	In paragraph 2, what do genes do? Why is this important?	
3.	How is GFP put into a mouse genome? Explain.	
4.	Why, in your opinion, would it be useful to put GFP into an animal genome?	

Self evaluation → I spoke 100% in English: ☐ Yes ☐ No

▸ Write what your instructor says. With a red pen, check.

----

7. Exercises

A. ▸ Think, write. Check with a red pen.

1. Recently, genome-based biotechnology has _____ rapidly.

2. In all organisms, DNA is _____ by children _____ their parents.

3. This means that genes are the resources for _____ proteins.

4. To do this, a GFP gene _____ from the jellyfish is put (or "_____") in…

5. This is called the CRISPR/Cas9 "_____" method.

B. ▸ Circle the correct answer. Check, and think of the reason.

1. The "genome" is (the / a) total genetic information of organisms.

2. GFP emits green fluorescence (when / then) it absorbs ultraviolet light.

3. Can you (explaining / explain) this figure?

4. CRISPR/Cas9 has enabled us to perform genome modification (quick / quickly).

5. This (is clear / clearly) indicates the ethical risks of this biotechnology.

C. ▸ Write the correct word form, and think of correct sentences.

a sequence (n)	→ (v) _____	an innovation (n)	→ (v) _____
to synthesize (v)	→ (n) a _____	a modification (n)	→ (v) _____

31

8. Translation

1. ゲノムは種によって異なることから、種の多様性はゲノムの多様性と言うことができる。
　　　　　　　　　　　　　　　　　＊ゲノムの多様性 species diversity

2. 下村脩博士はクラゲのゲノム中の緑色蛍光タンパク質を発見し単離したことによってノーベル賞を受賞した。 ＊緑色蛍光タンパク質 Green Fluorescent Protein,　＊単離したこと isolating

3. CRSPR/Cas9 の CRSPR は細菌のゲノム中に存在する繰り返し配列のことで、1987 年に日本人研究者によって発見された。　　　　　　　　　＊繰り返し配列 repeated sequences

4. 基礎研究によって得られた知見が、他の研究者によって応用されることで技術革新につながることが少なくない。　　　　　　　　　　＊技術革新 technological innovation

9. Writing

1. Write a summary of the text on p. 29. Include your feelings and ideas about the topic.

- - OR - -

2. Write an essay following your instructor's directions.

10. Extended reading and Review

▶ Search the Internet for related readings. What article did you choose? What is it about?

▶ Review this lesson. What *words*, *sentences*, or *ideas* are difficult? Why?

Lesson 9:　Mechatronics I

1. Vocabulary

▶ Listen and repeat. Memorize.

to refer	言及する	welding	溶接	situation	状態
motor	モーター	programmable	プログラム可能な	position	位置、ポジション
function	機能	instructions	指示、命令	limb	手足
to combine	一体化する	actuator	アクチュエーター 作動装置	correct	正しい
robot	ロボット	to judge	判断する		
industry	工業	to perform	行う、遂行する		
manufacturer	メーカー、製造業者	operation	操作、オペレーション		

2. Reading

▶ Read and study the text.

Mechatronics I

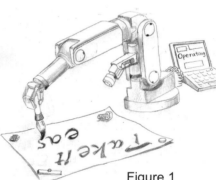

Figure 1

1　Mechatronics is a Japanese-English word. It refers to a system in which *motor function* and *control function* are combined. For example, look at Figure 1. This is a robot whose arms are moved by electric motors that are
5　controlled by a computer.

Mechatronic robots are used in many industries. For example, automobile manufacturers like Toyota use robots in their factories to make cars. Some robots move heavy parts, like the engine, into the car. Some do welding. Can you think of other things mechatronics or robots might
10　do?

Now let's take a closer look at mechatronic robots. First, the robot has a *programmable function*. This means you can program the computer to do something. The *microcomputer* (see Table 1) runs the
15　program. It makes the *actuator* of the machine move. Next, the machine can check its work. To do this, it uses a *sensor*. For example, the camera in Figure 1 checks what the machine
20　writes. Is the writing correct? If it is not correct, the machine will stop, or tell a human being that there is a problem.

Table 1

- Microcomputer (brains): It gives instructions to the actuators for motion. It judges information from the sensors.
- Actuator (limbs): It performs various operations under the microcomputer's control.
- Sensor (senses): It sends information from the outside (such as situation or position) to the microcomputer.

What is the robot in Figure 1 writing? How does it do it?　(Hint: start with the microcomputer)

3. Text notes

l.1: refer to 〜 「〜に関連している、〜を参照する、〜に言及する」

l.3: This is a robot whose arms are 〜 「これはロボットで、その（ロボットの）両腕は〜」

l.9: think of 〜 「〜を思いつく」

l.9: other things mechatronics or robots might do
「メカトロニクスやロボットができるかもしれない他のこと」

l.11: take a closer look at 〜 「もっと詳細に〜を見ていく」

4. Reading comprehension and Reading aloud

1. By yourself, or with a partner, answer these questions. Then check with the instructor.

▶ What are the main points of: *the first paragraph*? *the second*? *the third*? *the table*? *the fourth*?

I understand each paragraph: ☐ Yes ☐ Not yet

2. Now, with a partner, read the text aloud. Read smoothly, with good pronunciation.

▶ How was your reading and pronunciation? ☐ Good ☐ Needs more practice

5. Discussion

▶ Write, then ask. If you like, ask "follow-up" questions.

1. Have you ever seen or used a mechatronic robot? When? Where?	
2. What companies use mechatronic robots? (give examples!) To do what?	
3. What are the different parts of a mechatronic robot?	
4. How does the robot in Figure 1 work? (First it...then...next...)	
5. What is the difference between a mechatronic robot and a regular machine? Explain.	

Self evaluation → I spoke 100% in English: ☐ Yes ☐ No

6. Dictation

▶ Write what your instructor says. With a red pen, check.

----

7. Exercises

A. ▶ Think, write. Check with a red pen.

1. This is a robot whose arms _____ electric motors…

2. Some robots move heavy parts, _____ , into the car.

3. For example, the camera in Figure 1 checks _____ machine writes.

4. Actuator: It performs _____ under the microcomputer's control.

5. Sensor: It sends information from the outside (such as _____ or _____) to…

B. ▶ Circle the correct answer. Check, and think of the reason.

1. It refers to a system (for which / in which) motor function and control function are combined.

2. Automobile manufacturers like Toyota use robots in (them / their) factories to make cars.

3. Can you think of (other / another) things mechatronics or robots might do?

4. First, the robot has a (programmable / program) function.

5. Microcomputer: It gives instructions to the actuators (to / for) motion. It (judges / judging)…

C. ▶ Write the correct word form, and think of correct sentences.

to refer (v)	→	_(n) a_____		
industry (n)	→	_(adj)_____	→	_(v)_____
manufac-turer (n)	→	_(n)_____	→	_(v)_____

35

8. Translation

1. サポートディスクに相談する前に、マニュアルを詳細に見てみましょう。

2. そのマニュアルは、その機械の使い方やトラブルシューティングを私たちに示しています。

3. 私たちは、その機械に直線と曲線を描かせます。

4. もし問題があれば、販売元に機械を修理してもらうことができます。

9. Writing

1. Write a summary of the text on p. 33. Include your feelings and ideas about the topic.

- - OR - -

2. Write an essay following your instructor's directions.

----

10. Extended reading and Review

▶ Search the Internet for related articles. What article did you choose? What is it about?

▶ Review this lesson. What *words*, *sentences*, or *ideas* are difficult? Why?

Lesson 10: Using Ohm's law and Kirchhoff's laws

▶ Listen and repeat. Memorize.

to analyze	解析する	value	値、数値	conductance	コンダクタンス
circuit	回路	current	電流	equation	方程式
to flow	流れる	resistance	抵抗		

2. Reading

▶ Read and study the text, answer the questions.

Using Ohm's law and Kirchhoff's laws

1　You have learned about Ohm's law and Kirchhoff's laws in your engineering classes. Let's try to analyze an electric circuit by using these laws.

Using Ohm's Law

(1) Look at Figure 1. What is the value
5　of the current that flows into the resistance R?

Figure 1

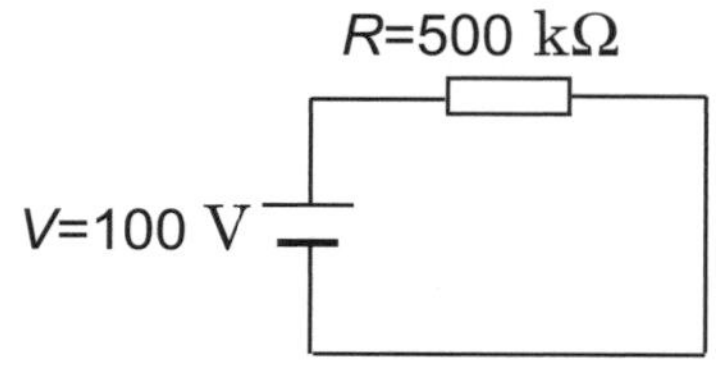

R=500 kΩ

V=100 V

(2) Look at Figure 2. A battery of 1.5 V is connected to the lamp. Then, the current becomes 0.3 A. What are the
10　values of the resistance and the conductance of the lamp?

Figure 2

I=0.3 A

Cell
(1.5 V)

Lamp

Using Kirchhoff's Current Law

(3) Look at Figure 3. What is the value of the current that flows into each
15　resistance?

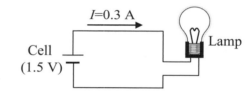

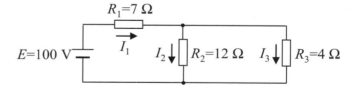

R_1=7 Ω

E=100 V　I_1　I_2↓ R_2=12 Ω　I_3↓ R_3=4 Ω

Figure 3

(Answers) ▶ Can you read the formulas below aloud in English?

(1) $I = \dfrac{V}{R} = \dfrac{100}{500 \times 10^3} = 0.2 \times 10^{-3}$ A $= 0.2$ mA

(2) $R = \dfrac{V}{I} = \dfrac{1.5}{0.3} = 5$ Ω　$G = \dfrac{1}{R} = \dfrac{1}{5} = 0.2$ S

(3) $I_1 = I_2 + I_3$,　$7I_1 + 12I_2 = 100$,　$-12I_2 + 4I_3 = 0$

$\rightarrow$　$I_1 = 10$ A, $I_2 = 2.5$ A, $I_3 = 7.5$ A

3. Text notes

I.1: Let's try to 〜 by …ing 「…することで〜してみよう」

Let's try to design the equipment by using computers.

（コンピューターを使ってその機器を設計してみよう。）

I.8: A is connected with B 「A は B と接続されている」

This PC is connected with the printer.

（この PC はそのプリンターとつながっている。）

4. Reading comprehension and Reading aloud

1. By yourself, or with a partner, answer these questions. Then check with the instructor.

▶ What are the main points of: *the first paragraph*? *the second*? *the third*? *the fourth*?

I understand each paragraph: ☐ Yes ☐ Not yet

2. Now, with a partner, read the text aloud. Read smoothly, with good pronunciation.

▶ How was your reading and pronunciation? ☐ Good ☐ Needs more practice

5. Discussion

▶ Write, then ask. If you like, ask "follow-up" questions.

1. Can you explain Figure 1? Do it. (Figure 1 shows a... In this circuit, the value of...)	
2. Can you explain Figure 2? Do it.	
3. Can you explain Figure 3? Do it.	
4. Do you think Ohm's law is a powerful law? Why? (*powerful = very useful*)	
5. Do you think Kirchhoff's laws are powerful laws? Why?	

Self evaluation → I spoke 100% in English: ☐ Yes ☐ No

6. Dictation

▶ Write what your instructor says. With a red pen, check.

----

7. Exercises

A.   ▶ Think, write. Check with a red pen.

1. You have learned about Ohm's law and Kirchhoff's laws in your _____...

2. Let's try _____ an _____ by using these laws.

3. What is the _____ of the current that _____ into the resistance R?

4. Look at Figure 2. A battery of 1.5 V is _____ the lamp.

5. Look at Figure 3. What is the value of the current that flows into each _____?

B.   ▶ Circle the correct answer. Check, and think of the reason.

1. You have learned about Ohm's law and Kirchhoff's (law / laws) in your engineering classes.

2. Let's try to (analyze / analyzes) an electric circuit by (use / using) these laws.

3. What is the value of the current that flows (into / onto) the resistance R?

4. What are the (values / value) of the resistance and the conductance of the lamp?

5. What is the value of (a / the) current that flows into each resistance?

C.   ▶ Write the correct word form, and think of correct sentences.

to analyze (v)   →   (n) an _____

conductance (n)   →   (v) _____

equation (n)   →   (v) _____

39

8. Translation

1. 私たちは電気回路図の描き方を学びました。

2. その回路図によると、蓄電池が２つの電灯とつながっています。

3. 電流の値はどのくらいですか。

4. 公式を使って電気回路の電圧と電流を計算する。

9. Writing

1. Write a summary of the text on p. 37. Include your feelings and ideas about the topic.

- - OR - -

2. Write an essay following your instructor's directions.

----

10. Extended reading and Review

▶ Search the Internet for related readings. What article did you choose? What is it about?

▶ Review this lesson. What *words*, *sentences*, or *ideas* are difficult? Why?

Lesson 11: F1 aerodynamics

1. Vocabulary

▶ Listen and repeat. Memorize.

aerodynamics	空気力学	flow	流れ、流動	to improve	向上する
abbreviation	略語	goal	目指すもの	common	一般的な
category	カテゴリー、部門	to decrease	減少させる	friction	摩擦
racing	競争	drag	抗力、空気抵抗	to obtain	得る
to increase	増加させる	opposite	反対	thrust	推進力
acceleration	加速度	direction	方向	wall	壁
stability	安定性	movement	運動	tunnel	トンネル

2. Reading

▶ Read and study the text.

F1 aerodynamics

1　　　F1 is an abbreviation of "Formula One". Formula One is the highest category of auto racing. Mechanical engineering and control engineering play very important roles in increasing the speed, acceleration and stability of Formula One cars. How?

Figure 1

5　　Let's look at aerodynamics. Aerodynamics is the study of the air flow around an object, for example, a car or an airplane. The goal of aerodynamics is to decrease *drag* (drag is the force which acts in the opposite direction of movement). Look at Figure 1. It shows the air flow around a wing. Decreasing drag force improves the performance of airplanes and cars. Toyota's *Prius* and Honda's *Insight* are examples of 10　good aerodynamic designs.

　　Do you think that formula cars have less drag force than common cars? The answer is 'no'. For formula cars, aerodynamics is used to increase *down-force*, not decrease drag force. Down force is the force that pushes a car to the 15　ground (Figure 2). Formula cars need a large *friction force* between the tires and the ground to obtain large *thrust force* and to corner with high speed. Down-force increases the friction and makes the formula car stable.

　　The large down-force of a formula car means that it can, 20　in theory, run on the wall of a tunnel! Can you explain the difference between drag and down-force?

Figure 2

3. Text notes

l.1: the highest category 「最高の領域（部門）」

l.3: play a(an) 〜 role 「〜な役割を果たす」

    The study of drag force plays an important role in making fast cars.

    （空気抵抗の研究は、速い車を作るために重要な役割を果たす。）

l.5: study 「研究」「学問」

l.11: less 〜 than … 「…より少ない〜」

l.14: the force that pushes a car to the ground 「車を地面に押す力」

l.17: to corner 「カーブを曲がる」

l.20: in theory 「理論上」「理屈の上では」

l.20: the difference between drag and down-force 「空気抵抗とダウンフォースとの違い（相違点）」

4. Reading comprehension and Reading aloud

1. By yourself, or with a partner, answer these questions. Then check with the instructor.

    ▶ What are the main points of: *the first paragraph*? *the second*? *the third*? *the fourth*?

        I understand each paragraph: ☐ Yes ☐ Not yet

2. Now, with a partner, read the text aloud. Read smoothly, with good pronunciation.

    ▶ How was your reading and pronunciation? ☐ Good ☐ Needs more practice

5. Discussion

▶ Write, then ask. If you like, ask "follow-up" questions.

1. What is Formula One? Do you like it? Why or why not?	
2. What is aerodynamics? Give two examples.	
3. What is drag? Why are Toyota and Nissan interested in aerodynamics?	
4. What is down-force? Why is it important?	

    Self evaluation →   I spoke 100% in English: ☐ Yes ☐ No

6. Dictation

▶ Write what your instructor says. With a red pen, check.

----

7. Exercises

A.　▶ Think, write. Check with a red pen.

1. F1 is an _____ of "Formula One".

2. Mechanical engineering … increase the speed, _____ and _____ …

3. Aerodynamics is_____ air flow around an object.

4. The goal of aerodynamics is to _____.

5. Down-force increases the _____ and makes the formula car _____.

B.　▶ Circle the correct answer. Check, and think of the reason.

1. Mechanical engineering and control engineering play very important (role / roles) in …

2. (drag is the force which acts in (a / the) opposite direction of movement).

3. Decreasing drag force improves the (performance / performing) of airplanes and cars.

4. Do you think (this / that) formula cars have less drag force than common cars?

5. The large down-force of a formula car means that it can, in (theory / theoretical), run on the…

C.　▶ Write the correct word form, and think of correct sentences.

aerodynamics (n)　→　(adj)_____

to increase (v)　→　(n) an_____

to decrease (v)　→　(n) a_____

43

8. Translation

1. 車は今日（こんにち）重要な役割を果たしている。

2. 車は私たちの日常生活を便利にする。　　　　＊日常の　daily

3. 重要なのは、安全な車を作ることだ。　　　（動名詞を用いて）

4. エンジニアは車の安全性能と環境性能の両方を向上させるために、日々研究をしている。

9. Writing

1. Write a summary of the text on p. 41, including your feelings and ideas.

- - OR - -

2. Write an essay following your instructor's directions.

----

10. Extended reading and Review

▶ Search the Internet for related articles. What article did you choose? What is it about?

▶ Review this lesson. What *words*, *sentences*, or *ideas* are difficult? Why?

Lesson 12: Applied chemistry: Creating instant ramen through sublimation

1. Vocabulary

▸ Listen and repeat. Memorize.

sublimation	昇華	phase	相，状態	diagram	図
discipline	（学問の）分野	to remove	除く	to vary	〜を変化させる
matter	物質	sanitary	衛生的な	conditions	状況
freeze-dried	フリーズドライ	vacuum	真空	to indicate	〜を示す
product	製品	pressure	圧力	to decrease	減少する
to spoil	傷む、腐る	relationship	関係	technique	技術
gaseous	気体の	substance	物質		

2. Reading

▸ Read and study the text.

Applied Chemistry: Creating instant ramen through sublimation

1   Chemistry is the discipline that studies and explores matter. In this lesson, we will look at the use of chemistry to create freeze-dried foods, like instant ramen and instant coffee. These products are very convenient, and do not spoil when they are on the shelves of a supermarket.

    As you know, the matter around us is usually in a solid, liquid, or gaseous phase. In order to
5   freeze dry ramen noodles, we need to remove the liquid water from the noodles, in a safe and sanitary way. We do this by freezing the noodles in a vacuum. This allows the water to change the phase (solid to gaseous), without passing through the liquid phase. This is called **sublimation**.

    How does this work? The phase of matter depends on temperature and pressure. A
10 diagram summarizing the relationship between the state of matter and temperature/pressure is called a "phase diagram". Figure 1 shows the phase diagram of water.

    Let us consider varying the temperature and
15 pressure conditions of water along the path shown in Figure 1. First, the water is in liquid form under the conditions at point X (1 atmospheric pressure and room temperature). As shown in Arrow 1, the temperature of the
20 water is decreased while keeping the pressure

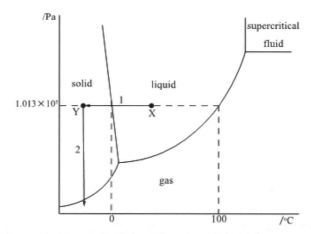

Figure 1. Phase diagram of water

constant, resulting in the conditions indicated at point Y. Next, the pressure is decreased as shown by Arrow 2 while keeping the temperature constant. Amazingly, the solid water then changes directly to gas, i.e., **sublimates**, without passing through a liquid phase.

    Can you explain Figure 1? This is the technology behind our instant ramen, and many other
25 products. Have you understood the technique? Can you explain what sublimation is?

3. Text notes

Title: Applied ～ 「応用～」

l.6: This allows the ～ 「直訳；これは～を許す 意訳；これにより～となる」

l.8: How does this work? 「どんな仕組みになっているだろうか？」

l.9: depends on ～ 「～に依存している」

l.12: Figure 1 shows ～ 「図１に～を示す」

l.14: Let us consider ～ 「～について考えてみよう」

l.17: 1 atmospheric pressure 「１気圧」

l.21: resulting in ～ 「その結果～」

l.23: i.e. ～ id est 「すなわち」（ラテン語から）

4. Reading comprehension and Reading aloud

1. By yourself, or with a partner, answer these questions. Then check with the instructor.

▶ What are the main points of: the *first paragraph*? the *second*? the *third*? the *fourth*? the *fifth*?

I understand each paragraph: ☐ Yes   ☐ Not yet

2. Now, with a partner, read the text aloud. Read smoothly, with good pronunciation.

▶ How was your reading and pronunciation? ☐ Good   ☐ Needs more practice

5. Discussion

▶ Write, then ask. If you like, ask "follow-up" questions.

1. Why are freeze-dried foods convenient?	
2. Why do you think freeze-drying is "sanitary"?	
3. Explain Figure 1 (First,… Then,…)	
4. What is sublimation (in chemistry)?	

Self evaluation →   I spoke 100% in English: ☐ Yes   ☐ No

46

▶ Write what your instructor says. With a red pen, check.

----

7. Exercises

A.   ▶ Think, write. Check with a red pen.

1. These products are very _____ , and do not _____ when they are on…

2. The matter around us is usually in a _____ , _____ , or _____ phase.

3. We need to remove the liquid water from the noodles, in a safe and _____ way.

4. The phase of matter _____ temperature and pressure.

5. Amazingly, the solid water then changes _____ to gas,…

B.   ▶ Circle the correct answer. Check, and think of the reason.

1. Chemistry is the discipline (what / that) studies and explores matter.

2. In order to freeze dry ramen noodles, we need to (remove / removing) the liquid water from…

3. We do this by (freezes / freezing) the noodles (in / under) a vacuum.

4. A diagram (to summarize / summarizing) the relationship between the temperature and…

5. Next, the pressure is decreased as (shown / showing) by Arrow 2 while keeping the…

C.   ▶ Write the correct word form, and think of correct sentences.

sublimation (n)   →   (v) _____

sanitary (adj)   →   (v) _____

pressure (n)   →   (v) _____

8. Translation

1. この実験結果は目的の分子が生成していることを示唆している（示している）。

2. 表1に測定の結果を示した。

3. 温度と圧力の関係を調査した。

4. 温度を変化させて実験を行った。

9. Writing

1. Write a summary of the text on p. 45. Include your feelings and ideas about the topic.

- - OR - -

2. Write an essay following your instructor's directions.

----

10. Extended reading and Review

▶ Search the Internet for related readings. What article did you choose? What is it about?

▶ Review this lesson. What *words*, *sentences*, or *ideas* are difficult? Why?

Lesson 13:   Mechatronics II

1. Vocabulary

▶ Listen and repeat. Memorize.

to participate	参加する	lift	持ち上げる、揚力	precise	正確な
specific	特定の	force	力	to develop	開発する
technique	技術、テクニック	angle	角度	to compete	競争する
to collect	収集する、集める	parameter	パラメーター	clumsy	ぎこちない
model	モデル	stable	安定した	motion	動き
technology	技術、テクノロジー	location	場所	feedback	フィードバック
to mimic	模倣する、真似をする	pressure	圧力	shape	形状、形
flippers	足ひれ				

2. Reading

▶ Read and study the text.

Mechatronics II

1   Students of technology can participate in robot contests (or Robocons) in Japan, and internationally. There are many types of contests. Today, we will talk about a contest for swimming robots. Specifically, we will look at a sea turtle robot.

To make a turtle robot, we first need to understand how a turtle swims. By using an *image data*
5 *processing* technique, we can collect information to make a simple kinetic model of a swimming turtle.

Next, how do we create the technologies to mimic how a turtle swims? Please look at photos 1 and 2. These are research models that use a PIC microcomputer to control a DC servo motor. This motor moves the wing-shaped flippers. The flippers can be made to wag fast or slow, and this
10 makes a strong lift force to move the turtle forward.

Lift force is related to the second power of velocity, so the wag speed and the angle of the flippers are important parameters to make the swimming stable and faster. Moreover, the positioning of the sensors to measure speed, location, and pressure is very important so that the microcomputer can precisely control the motor.

15 These research models are being developed in order to compete in an underwater robot contest. Usually, when we first make a robot the movements are a little clumsy.

Therefore, we must improve the motion of the flippers, the feedback from the sensors, the shape of the robot, and so on. So
20 teamwork is very important in order to win. Would you like to be on a team and compete?

1. Sea turtle robot   2. Dolphin robot
(photos © Kazunori Hosotani)

3. Text notes

l.1: participate in 〜 = take part in 〜 「〜に参加する、〜に出席する」

l.2: types of 〜 = kinds of 〜 「数種類の〜、いくつかの種類の〜」

l.4: By using 〜 「〜を使うことによって、〜を利用することにより」（前置詞＋動名詞）

l.8: PIC = Peripheral Interface Controller 「ピック」

l.9: the wing-shaped flippers 「翼の形をした足ひれ」

l.11: be related to 〜 「〜に関連している、〜に関係している」

l.19: and so on 「〜など」

l.21: would you like to 〜 「〜したいですか？、〜するのはいかがですか？」（疑問文）

　　　← you would like to 〜 （肯定文）

4. Reading comprehension and Reading aloud

1. By yourself, or with a partner, answer these questions. Then check with the instructor.

▶ What are the main points of: *the first paragraph*? *the second*? *the third*? *the fourth*? *the fifth*?

I understand each paragraph: ☐ Yes ☐ Not yet

2. Now, with a partner, read the text aloud. Read smoothly, with good pronunciation.

▶ How was your reading and pronunciation? ☐ Good ☐ Needs more practice

5. Discussion

▶ Write, then ask. If you like, ask "follow-up" questions.

1. Do you like Robocons? Why?	
2. How does the "Sea turtle robot" swim? Explain.	
3. How can the "lift force" be controlled and modified? Explain.	
4. What do the sensors measure? Where do you think the sensors are?	
5. What did they do to improve the "Sea turtle robot"?	

Self evaluation → I spoke 100% in English: ☐ Yes ☐ No

6. Dictation

▸ Write what your instructor says. With a red pen, check.

----

7. Exercises

A.   ▸ Think, write. Check with a red pen.

1. Students of technology can _____ robot contests in Japan.

2. To make a turtle robot, we first need to _____ a turtle swims.

3. How do we create the technologies to _____ a turtle swims?

4. The positioning of sensors to measure _____ , _____ , and pressure is…

5. Therefore, we must _____ motion of the flippers, the feedback from…

B.   ▸ Circle the correct answer. Check, and think of the reason.

1. Students … can participate in robot contests in Japan, and (international / internationally).

2. By using an image data processing technique, we can (collect / correct) information to…

3. …and this makes a strong lift force to move (the / a) turtle forward.

4. …so the wag speed and (the / an) angle of (the / a) knee are important parameters to…

5. Usually, when we first make (the / a) robot the movements are a little clumsy.

C.   ▸ Write the correct word form, and think of correct sentences.

to partici-pate (v)	→	(n) _____		
stable (adj)	→	(n) _____	→	(v) _____
precise (adj)	→	(n) _____	→	(adv) _____

51

8. Translation

1. 私の夢は大学に進み、学生ロボコンに参加することだ。

2. だから、大学に入ることができるように、今一生懸命勉強している。

3. また、ロボットに関連する科目を勉強することにより、専門知識を身につけている。

4. あなたもメカトロニクスを学びたいですか。

9. Writing

1. Write a summary of the text on p. 49. Include your feelings and ideas about the topic.

- - OR - -

2. Write an essay following your instructor's directions.

10. Extended reading and Review

▶ Search the Internet for related readings. What article did you choose? What is it about?

▶ Review this lesson. What *words*, *sentences*, or *ideas* are difficult? Why?

Lesson 14: Information literacy

▶ Listen and repeat. Memorize.

literacy	読み書き能力 リテラシー	professional	職業の、プロの	effectively	効果的に
ability	能力	journal	機関誌、雑誌	to surround	取り巻く、囲む
to identify	見つける	reliable	信頼できる	network	ネットワーク
source	源、出所	current	現在の	security	安全
to evaluate	評価する	bias	偏り	to expose	（危険などに）さらす
critically	決定的に	issue	問題、論点	threat	脅威
knowledge	知識	society	社会、学会	infection	感染
search	探す	to interact	協力しあう	attachment	付着物、添付物

2. Reading

▶ Read and study the text.

Information literacy

1 Information literacy is the ability to identify what information you need, find the best sources of information, evaluate those sources critically, and share the information. For example, if you need information about engine design, you need to be able to search professional reports, journals, and other sources. By doing this, your knowledge base will grow. You will be able to understand current

5 issues in technology and society, and you can interact effectively at college and work.

Information literacy is very important because we are surrounded by a growing network of information. However, there can be problems. Not all information is created equal: some is reliable and current, but some is biased, out of date, misleading, or simply false.

Moreover, there are security problems. Networked computers are exposed to the threat of viruses

10 all the time. Your computers can be attacked through your network even though they are password-protected. For example, virus infection can occur through security holes in the Operating System (OS). Viruses can also infect your computers through e-mail attachments and downloaded free software. Once a computer is infected with a virus, the computer may spread the virus to other computers, or send thousands of spam mails. Therefore, knowing about security technology is

15 another important part of information literacy.

In conclusion, it is necessary for us to become information literate, so that we can participate in the world of information and research, and understand security issues as well.

3. Text notes

l.1: the ability to ① identify ～, ② find ～, ③ evaluate ～, and ④ share～.
「①、②、③、④の４つをする能力」

l.4: your knowledge base 「知識の基」

l.8: out of date 「時代遅れの」「旧式の」 ↔ up to date 「現代の」「最新式の」

l.9: be exposed to ～ 「～にさらされている」

l.10: all the time 「いつでも」「ずっと」

l.14: thousands of ～ 「何千もの～」「たくさんの～」
（hundreds of ～: 何百もの～、 millions of ~: 何百万もの～）

l.14: spam mails 「迷惑メール」「スパムメール」

l.16: in conclusion 「結果として」

l.17: as well 「同様に」「～もまた」

4. Reading comprehension and Reading aloud

1. By yourself, or with a partner, answer these questions. Then check with the instructor.

▸ What are the main points of: *the first paragraph*? *the second*? *the third*? *the fourth*?

I understand each paragraph: ☐ Yes ☐ Not yet

2. Now, with a partner, read the text aloud. Read smoothly, with good pronunciation.

▸ How was your reading and pronunciation? ☐ Good ☐ Needs more practice

5. Discussion

▸ Write, then ask. If you like, ask "follow-up" questions.

1. In your opinion, what does "information literacy" mean?	
2. Why is "information literacy" important when you do research?	
3. Think about your "knowledge base". Where are you strong? Not strong?	
4. How can we improve our information literacy? (give examples)	

Self evaluation → I spoke 100% in English: ☐ Yes ☐ No

6. Dictation

▶ Write what your instructor says. With a red pen, check.

----

7. Exercises

A.　▶ Think, write. Check with a red pen.

1. Information literacy is the ability to identify _____ information you need,…

2. …you need to _____ search professional reports, journals, and other sources.

3. By doing this, your _____ will grow.

4. Not all information is created equal: some is…, but some is _____ , out of date,…

5. Networked computers are _____ of viruses all the time.

B.　▶ Circle the correct answer. Check, and think of the reason.

1. Information literacy is the ability to …, evaluate those sources (critically / critical), and…

2. You will be able to understand…, and you can interact (effective / effectively) at college and…

3. Information literacy is very important (moreover / because) we are surrounded by…

4. Your computers can be (attacked / attack) through your network even though they are…

5. Therefore, (to know / knowing) about security technology is another important part of…

C.　▶ Write the correct word form, and think of correct sentences.

to evaluate (v)　→　(n) an _____

reliable (adj)　→　(n) _____

infection (n)　→　(v) _____

55

8. Translation

1. 彼は毎日何百通もの e-mail を受け取る。

2. 実は、彼はそのすべてのメールを読んでいるわけではない。

3. 彼は自分のコンピューターがウィルスに感染するのではないかとおそれて、いくつかのメールを開かないことがある。

4. その結果、重要な情報を見逃して仕事上の支障が生じることがある。

9. Writing

1. Write a summary of the text on p. 53. Include your feelings and ideas about the topic.

- - OR - -

2. Write an essay following your instructor's directions.

10. Extended reading and Review

▶ Search the Internet for related readings. What article did you choose? What is it about?

▶ Review this lesson. What *words*, *sentences*, or *ideas* are difficult? Why?

Lesson 15: When "information recommendation" meets AI

1. Vocabulary

▶ Listen and repeat. Memorize.

recommendation	推薦	boom	爆発、ブーム	text	文書
frequently	頻繁に	to enhance	強める	to establish	確立する
to launch	公開する	accumulation	蓄積	to recognize	識別する
service	サービス	profile	プロフィール	mathematical	数学的
collaborative	協調	to rank	ランキングする	to purchase	購買
to filter	濾過する				

2. Reading

▶ Read and study the text.

When "information recommendation" meets Artificial Intelligence

1 When you want to buy something on the internet, the website frequently *recommends* products for you to consider. For example, it may recommend books, or new computer games. Do you think this is useful? Many people think it is useful, and it is called "information recommendation".

5 In 1998, Amazon launched its first service to recommend similar products to users. It was based on a simple matrix calculation algorithm, called "collaborative filtering" (CF). Please study Fig. 1. Can you
10 understand how CF works? It is reported that about 30 percent of the page views at Amazon.com are now from recommendations.

History ratings	$user_1$	$user_2$	$user_3$	$user_4$	$user_5$	$user_6$	$user_7$
$product_1$	5			1	1	Step 2 similarity	
$product_2$		1	5	4	5		4
$product_3$			2			1	Step 3
$product_4$	2	4		5			?

Step 1

Fig. 1. A collaborative filtering matrix.

15 Nowadays, "big data" and the Artificial Intelligence (AI) boom are enhancing information recommendation a lot. Recommender systems take advantage of both the huge accumulated amount of data and massively parallel computing to construct user profiles. To do this, it uses not only the history rankings, but also text and photographs as well. In short, machine learning, one of the AI techniques, has mainly taken the place of CF. It establishes a mathematical model and recognizes the patterns in a user's purchase habits with time, season, even the sequence in
20 which the user buys the products. Thus, it provides more precise results than traditional CF in order to make recommendations.

In sum, the new recommender systems may understand you better than you do! Can you explain how CF and AI based recommender systems work?

3. Text notes

Title: information recommendation 「情報推薦」

I.10: It is reported that 〜 「〜と報告されている」

I.12: page views 「ページの閲覧」

I.15: take advantage of 〜 「〜 を取り入れる」

I.16: massively parallel computing 「大規模並列処理」

I.16: user profiles 「ユーザープロファイル」

I.19: purchase habits 「購買習慣」

4. Reading comprehension and Reading aloud

1. By yourself, or with a partner, answer these questions. Then check with the instructor.

   ▸ What are the main points of: *the first paragraph*? *the second*? *the third*? *the fourth*?

   I understand each paragraph: ☐ Yes ☐ Not yet

2. Now, with a partner, read the text aloud. Read smoothly, with good pronunciation.

   ▸ How was your reading and pronunciation? ☐ Good ☐ Needs more practice

5. Discussion

▸ Write, then ask. If you like, ask "follow-up" questions.

1. Do you use websites that use recommender systems? Which ones? Do you like the systems? Why?	
2. What does CF mean? Explain Table 2 ("In the table, the top axis is… Then Step 1 is…").	
3. The text says that AI "has mainly taken the place of CF". How? Explain.	
4. In summary, explain how AI based recommender systems work.	

Self evaluation →   I spoke 100% in English: ☐ Yes ☐ No

6. Dictation

▶ Write what your instructor says. With a red pen, check.

----

7. Exercises

A.　▶ Think, write. Check with a red pen.

1. It was based on a simple … algorithm, called "_____".

2. It is reported that about 30 percent of the _____ at Amazon.com are…

3. Nowadays, "big data" and the AI boom are _____ information…

4. Recommender systems take advantage of … to construct "_____".

5. In short, machine learning… has mainly _____ of CF.

B.　▶ Circle the correct answer. Check, and think of the reason.

1. Many people think it is useful, (and / though) it is called "Information Recommendation".

2. In 1998, Amazon (has launched / launched) its first service to recommend products to users.

3. Can you understand (that / how) CF works?

4. Recommender systems take (advantage / advantages) of both the huge…

5. Thus, it provides more (precision / precise) results than traditional CF.

C.　▶ Write the correct word form, and think of correct sentences.

to enhance (v)　　　→　(n) an _____

an accumulation (n)　→　(v) _____

to recognize (v)　　　→　(n) _____

8. Translation

1. 協調フィルタリングでも、機械学習の手法でも、ユーザーのデータに基づく。

2. ユーザーのプロフィールはビッグデータとして活用され、システムが正確な予測を行う。

3. もし旅行の目的地に迷っているなら、観光推薦システムを使うのが良いアイデアです。

   ＊観光　sightseeing

4. この商品を買った人はこれらの商品も買っている。

9. Writing

1. Write a summary of the text on p. 57. Include your feelings and ideas about the topic.

- - OR - -

2. Write an essay following your instructor's directions.

10. Extended reading and Review

▶ Search the Internet for related readings. What article did you choose? What is it about?

▶ Review this lesson. What *words*, *sentences*, or *ideas* are difficult? Why?

Lesson 16:   Space junk: The problem of waste in space

1. Vocabulary

▶ Listen and repeat. Memorize.

waste	廃棄物	typical	典型的な	to break up	分裂する、離散する
space	宇宙空間	therefore	それゆえ	to spread	拡散する、広がる
satellite	人工衛星	relative	相対的な	cloud	雲
piece	1片、1個	velocity	速度	diameter	直径
to orbit	周回する	impact	衝突	to monitor	監視する、モニターする
useless	無駄な、不要な	vehicle	(宇宙)船、輸送手段	agency	(政府)機関
debris	デブリ、破片	to destroy	破壊する	collision	衝突
junk	ガラクタ	kinetic	運動の	to track	追跡する
to travel	移動する	related to	～に関連した	to discuss	議論する

2. Reading

▶ Read and study the text.

Space junk: The problem of waste in space

1   As you know, we have a problem of too much waste on the earth. But did you know that we have a problem of too much waste in space too? There are many old satellites and pieces of old space equipment that are orbiting the earth. They are useless. They are called "space debris", or just "space junk". Today, we will talk about why this space junk is a big problem.

5   First problem: space junk travels at a very high speed. A typical piece of space junk travels at about 7-8km/s. Therefore, the relative velocity on impact may be 10km/s. Think about that speed - how far does a fast car travel in 1 second? A jet? Can you imagine 7-8km/s? If this piece of space junk hits another space vehicle it will damage or destroy that vehicle, even if the piece is very small. As you know, kinetic energy is related to the second power of velocity, as shown in the equation:

$$E = \frac{1}{2}MV^2 \quad [\text{kg}\cdot\text{m}^2/\text{s}^2] \text{ or } [\text{N}\cdot\text{m}] \text{ or } [\text{ J }]$$

10   Second problem: when old satellites break up, many small parts, or debris, which also travel at high speed, will spread in space. These small parts also break up, over and over, and finally create a *debris cloud* as shown in Figure 1.

Figure 1.

15   Today, all pieces of debris of 10cm or more in diameter are monitored by agencies like NASA and JAXA, in order to avoid collisions. How do you think NASA tracks all this junk? It's difficult! We will discuss this and other space issues in future lessons. But for now, please review what you have learned about space debris.

[Problem] Estimate the kinetic energy of a small piece of space debris (*M*=1kg, *V*=10km/s).

3. Text notes

I.5: travel 「（光や音などが）伝わる」

Light travels faster than sound. （光は音よりも速く伝わる。）

I.8: even if ～ 「たとえ～であるとしても」

I.9: be related to ～ 「～に関係がある、～に関心を持つ」

EQUATION: *E* equals one-half *M V* squared kilogram m (meter) squared per s (second) squared or Newton meter or Joule.

I.11: many small parts, or debris (which also travel at high speed) will spread in space.

「多くの小さな成分が、即ち破片が、（その破片もまた高速で移動している）宇宙空間に散布するのである。」

I.13: over and over 「何度も何度も」

I.17: How do you think NASA tracks all this junk?

How does NASA track all this junk? + Do you think?

I.18: for now 「さしあたり、今のところ」

4. Reading comprehension and Reading aloud

1. By yourself, or with a partner, answer these questions. Then check with the instructor.

▶ What are the main points of: *the first paragraph*? *the second*? *the third*? *the fourth*?

I understand each paragraph: ☐ Yes ☐ Not yet

2. Now, with a partner, read the text aloud. Read smoothly, with good pronunciation.

▶ How was your reading and pronunciation? ☐ Good ☐ Needs more practice

5. Discussion

▶ Write, then ask. If you like, ask "follow-up" questions.

1. What is the typical speed (V) of a piece of space junk? Why is it dangerous?	
2. What is a "debris cloud?" Explain. How does it happen?	
3. How do you think JAXA tracks space junk? Explain.	
4. Would you like to track space junk? Why?	

Self evaluation → I spoke 100% in English: ☐ Yes ☐ No

▸ Write what your instructor says. With a red pen, check your work.

----

7. Exercises

A. ▸ Think, write. Check with a red pen.

1. There are many old satellites and pieces of old _____ that are...

2. Today, we will talk about _____ this space junk is a big problem.

3. If this piece of space junk hits another space vehicle it will damage or _____ that vehicle.

4. When old satellites _____ up, many small parts, or _____ , which also...

5. Today, all pieces of debris of 10cm or more in diameter are _____ by...

B. ▸ Circle the correct answer. Check, and think of the reason.

1. There are many old (satellite / satellites) and (pieces / piece) of old space equipment that...

2. Think about that speed - how far does (a / the) fast car travel in 1 second?

3. ...it will damage or destroy that vehicle, (even if / even as) the piece is very small.

4. These small parts also break up, over and over, and (final / finally) create a debris cloud as...

5. Today, all pieces of debris of 10cm or more in diameter are monitored (on / by) agencies like...

C. ▸ Write the correct word form, and think of correct sentences.

typical (adj)   →   (adv) _____

to destroy (v) →   (n) _____

a collision (n) →   (v) _____

8. Translation

1. 私が今習っていることは、ロボットと関連がある。

2. たとえそれが難しくても、私はロボット技師になるつもりだ。

3. 先生が言われるように、何度も何度も教科書を復習している。

4. どうやったら私は次の試験で良い点を取れると思いますか。

9. Writing

1. Write a summary of the text on p. 61. Include your feelings and ideas about the topic.

- - *OR* - -

2. Write an essay following your instructor's directions.

----

10. Extended reading and Review

▶ Search the Internet for related readings. What article did you choose? What is it about?

▶ Review this lesson. What *words*, *sentences*, or *ideas* are difficult? Why?

Lesson 17:   Air pollution and control technology

1. Vocabulary

▶ Listen and repeat. Memorize.

pollution	汚染	to release	放出する	pollutants	汚染物質
serious	深刻な	damage	被害、ダメージ	atmosphere	大気
environmental	環境の	to reduce	減らす、減少する	to improve	良くする、良くなる
to face	直面する	development	開発	hazardous	危険な
various	さまざまな	effort	努力	photochemical	光化学の
carbon	炭素	citizen	市民	smog	スモッグ
monoxide	一酸化物	economic	経済の、経済上の	solvent	溶剤、溶媒
dioxin	ダイオキシン	growth	成長	dry cleaning	ドライクリーニング
moreover	さらに	to regulate	規制する	chlorination	塩素処理

2. Reading

▶ Read and study the text.

Air pollution and control technology

1   Air pollution is a serious environmental problem facing us today, and the causes are the activities of us human beings. There are various types of air pollution, for example, carbon monoxide from gasoline burning cars, and dioxin from burning trash. Moreover, we release a huge amount of carbon dioxide (CO_2) from burning coal and liquefied natural gas (LNG) to generate electricity, 5   which causes global warming.

There are many factories in Japan, and these factories caused serious environmental damage in the 1960s and 1970s. Today, the amount of serious air pollution has been reduced by the development of earth-friendly technology and individual efforts by citizens. On the other hand, air pollution is still a serious problem in Asia, 10   especially in areas of high economic growth or in areas where there is a population explosion. In many cases, air pollution from factories and vehicles in these regions is not effectively regulated.

15   Please look at Table 1. It shows some of the worst pollutants in cities with factories. Since these pollutants are still released in Japan and around the world, we must continue our efforts to reduce all pollutants.

Table 1.   Hazardous air pollutants

Nitrogen Oxides (NOx)	From factories, vehicles, power plants → causes photochemical smog and acid rain.
Sulfur Oxides (SOx)	
Benzene	From solvents used in industry, and for dry cleaning, or in the chlorination of propane.
Tri-chloro-ethylene	
Tetra-chloro-ethylene	
Di-chloro-methane	

20   Reducing the amount of CO_2 released into the atmosphere is one of the biggest challenges today. The technology you study is very important in order to improve many environmental problems, including air pollution and global warming.

3. Text notes

l.2: us human beings 　「私たち人間」

l.3: a huge amount of 〜 　「多大な〜」「莫大な〜」

　　 cf.) a large [small] amount of 〜 　「多量の［少量の］〜」

l.5: which causes global warming

　「それ（莫大な量の二酸化炭素）は、地球温暖化を引き起こしている」

l.7: in the 1960s and 1970s 　「1960 年代と 1970 年代に」

l.7: has been reduced 　「減らされてきている」

l.8: on the other hand 　「その一方で」

l.11: in areas where there is a population explosion 　「人口爆発がある地域では」

l.16: worst 　「一番ひどい」「最悪な」

l.20: Reducing the amount of CO_2 　「二酸化炭素の量を減らすことは」

l.21: The technology you study 　「あなた達が勉強している技術は」

4. Reading comprehension and Reading aloud

1. By yourself, or with a partner, answer these questions. Then check with the instructor.

▸ What are the main points of: *the first paragraph*? *the second*? *the third*? *the fourth*?

　　　　　I understand each paragraph: 　☐ Yes 　☐ Not yet

2. Now, with a partner, read the text aloud. Read smoothly, with good pronunciation.

▸ How was your reading and pronunciation? 　☐ Good 　☐ Needs more practice

5. Discussion

▸ Write, then ask. If you like, ask "follow-up" questions.

1. What are some examples of air pollution? From what?	
2. Why is air pollution a problem? For example?	
3. Why is CO_2 a problem? Explain.	
4. What are some common pollutants? Where do they come from?	

Self evaluation → 　　　I spoke 100% in English: 　☐ Yes 　☐ No

6. Dictation

▶ Write what your instructor says. With a red pen, check.

----

7. Exercises

A. ▶ Think, write. Check with a red pen.

1. Air pollution is a serious _____ facing us today.

2. There are various types of air pollution, for example, _____ from cars.

3. Air pollution is still a serious problem in Asia, especially in areas of high _____ growth.

4. Reducing the amount of CO_2 _____ the atmosphere is one of the biggest...

5. Benzene - From solvents used in industry,... or in the _____ of propane.

B. ▶ Circle the correct answer. Check, and think of the reason.

1. Air pollution is a serious environmental problem (facing / to face) us today.

2. Today, the amount of serious air pollution (has been / is been) reduced by the development of...

3. On the other hand, air pollution is (though / still) a serious problem in Asia, especially in...

4. Please look at Table 1. It shows some of the worst (pollutant / pollutants) in cities with factories.

5. Nitrogen Oxides (NOx) - From cars, causes (photochemistry / photochemical) smog or acid rain.

C. ▶ Write the correct word form.

growth (n)   → (v) _____

to improve (v)   → (n) an _____

chlorination (n) → (v) _____

67

8. Translation

1. 現在、私たちは様々な環境問題に直面している。

2. 私たちは毎日多量のプラスチックを使っている。

3. 私たちが使うプラスチックは、ゴミ問題を引き起こしている。　　＊ゴミ問題　trash problem

4. 　ゴミの量を減らすことは、地球環境にとって重要である。

9. Writing

1. Write a summary of the text on p. 65. Include your feelings and ideas about the topic.

- - *OR* - -

2. Write an essay following your instructor's directions.

----

10. Extended reading and Review

▶ Search the Internet for related readings. What article did you choose? What is it about?

▶ Review this lesson. What *words*, *sentences*, or *ideas* are difficult? Why?

Lesson 18:   Airbus vs. Boeing

▶ Listen and repeat. Memorize.

mainstream	主流	passenger	乗客	to evolve	進化する
demand	需要	range	航続距離	workload	作業量
order	受注	operation	運用	pace	勢い
strategy	戦略	century	世紀	factor	要因
capacity	容量（ここでは数）	to earn	獲得する	to motivate	動機付ける

2. Reading

▶ Read and study the text.

Airbus vs. Boeing

1   In the past, large aircraft were the mainstream in the aircraft market, but in recent years smaller aircraft, like the A320neo and the B737MAX, have become more popular. The reasons for this are increasing passenger demand for frequent flights, as well as the requirement to reduce the costs for fuel and to reduce CO_2 emissions. As a result, the number of orders for large B747-8 and A380

5   aircraft has dropped to zero. On the other hand, demand for small aircraft keeps increasing, thus orders for small aircraft accounted for 94% of Airbus's total orders for 1,078 aircraft in FY2022. The situation is the same for Boeing, with the smaller aircraft accounting for 72% of the total orders for 774 aircraft in FY2022.

10   Let's take a look at the differences in strategy for small aircraft between Airbus and Boeing. Airbus currently offers the A320neo (standard seating capacity: 150-180 passengers) and A321neo (standard seating capacity: 180-220) families, based on the A320 series launched in the late 1980s. These aircraft have been continuously improved for efficiency and fuel consumption. Though small aircraft are generally associated with short-haul routes, the A321XLR (Xtra Long

15   Range) will have a range of 4,700 NM (approx. 8,700 km). This means the A321XLR will be able to fly nonstop from Tokyo to the West Coast of the United States, or to Australia, or Eastern Europe.

On the other hand, with the 737MAX family, Boeing is competing with Airbus. The 737 series has been the best-selling aircraft in the world since its first flight in 1967. The 737 series has a standard seating range of 138-230 seats, and a maximum range of 3,825 NM (approx. 7,084 km). Because

20   the aircraft has been in operation for more than half a century, it has earned the trust of airlines and pilots, and design and engine improvements have continuously made it more efficient. Moreover, the cockpit layout has been progressively evolving, adopting the glass cockpit similar to that of 787 series, Boeing's latest aircraft, which reduces workload of pilots.

Worldwide demand for small aircraft is growing at an unstoppable pace, as shown by the United

25   Airlines order for 100 737MAX family aircraft in December 2022, as well as Air India's order for 210 A320 family aircraft in February 2023. Thus, airline companies like ANA and United have to decide between aircraft like the A320neo and the B737MAX. What factors (discussed in this article) do you think motivate their decision-making?

69

3. Text notes

l.3: passenger demand 「旅客需要」 reduce the costs for ～「～のためのコストを削減する」
l.6: account for ～ 「～をも占める」
l.7: in FY2022 「2022 会計年度」（FY = fiscal year）
l.12: launched in the late 1980s 「1980 年代末期に初飛行した」
l.13: fuel consumption 「燃料消費」
l.14: short-haul routes 「短距離路線」
l.21: improvements have continuously made it more efficient「継続的に効率化を図る」
l.22: the cockpit layout has been progressively evolving「コックピットレイアウトは、どんどん進化し」
l.22: glass cockpit「グラスコックピット」（In the cockpit, all LCDs, no older-style gauges.）
l.27: What factors…motivate their decision-making?
　　「どのような要因が…の意思決定の動機となっているか?」

4. Reading comprehension and Reading aloud

1. By yourself, or with a partner, answer these questions. Then check with the instructor.

▸ What are the main points of: *the first paragraph*? *the second*? *the third*? *the fourth*?

I understand each paragraph: ☐ Yes ☐ Not yet

2. Now, with a partner, read the text aloud. Read smoothly, with good pronunciation.

▸ How was your reading and pronunciation? ☐ Good ☐ Needs more practice

5. Discussion

▸ Write, then ask. If you like, ask "follow-up" questions.

1. What are B747-8 and A380 airplanes? Why has the number of orders dropped to zero?	
2. What are the smaller aircraft discussed in this article? What are the number of orders? Why have they increased?	
3. Compare the A320neo and B737MAX aircraft.	
4. When airlines decide to buy aircraft, what factors motivate their decision-making?	

Self evaluation → I spoke 100% in English: ☐ Yes ☐ No

6. Dictation

▶ Write what your instructor says. With a red pen, check.

----

7. Exercises

A.   ▶ Think, write. Check with a red pen.

1. In the past, large aircraft were the _____ in the aircraft _____.

2. The reasons for this are increasing passenger _____ for frequent flights,…

3. Though small aircraft are generally associated with _____ routes, the A321XLR…

4. These aircraft have been continuously _____ efficiency and…

5. Worldwide demand for small aircraft is growing at an _____,…

B.   ▶ Circle the correct answer. Check, and think of the reason.

1. In the past, large aircraft (was / were) the mainstream in the aircraft market.

2. Let's take a look at the differences (in / on) strategy for small aircraft between Airbus and…

3. Airbus (currency / currently) offers the A320neo (standard seating capacity: 150-180) and…

4. Because the aircraft has been (in / on) operation for more than half a century,…

5. What factors (discussed in…) do you think (motivating / motivate) their decision-making?

C.   ▶ Write the correct word form, and think of correct sentences.

strategy (n)   → _(adj)_ _____

operation (n)   → _(v)_ _____

to motivate (v) → _(n)_ _____

8. Translation

1. ボーイング製の飛行機は、世界の旅客機の60%を占める。

2. この自動車の定員は、8人です。

3. 自動運転技術は、運転者の作業量を軽減している。

4. 効率性を追求する需要の増加は、とどまるところを知らない。

9. Writing

1. Write a summary of the text on p. 69. Include your feelings and ideas about the topic.

- - OR - -

2. Write an essay following your instructor's directions.

----

10. Extended reading and Review

▶ Search the Internet for related readings. What article did you choose? What is it about?

▶ Review this lesson. What *words*, *sentences*, or *ideas* are difficult? Why?

Lesson 1: Advanced science *and* Mechanical engineering

工学の世界には多くの分野があり、機械工学、電気工学、コンピューター工学、化学工学などがあります。しかし、20世紀末から、遺伝子工学のような新しい分野が誕生しました。

新しい分野の誕生によって、先端科学はエンジニアリングの中でさらに重要な位置を占めるようになりました。先端科学には、数学、生物学、化学、物理学が含まれます。前述したように、これらは多くの新しい学際的分野（分野を超えた融合的な学問分野）に発展しています。したがって、精密測定などの先端科学のスキルは、すべての工学・技術分野において重要となっています。

機械工学は機械と材料に関する学問分野です。機械工学は、最も古い工学分野のひとつです。すべての機械は機械工学に基づいて設計されています。例えば、自動車にはエンジンまたはモーター、トランスミッション、ブレーキ、車体があります。これらはいずれも機械工学に基づいて設計されています。

機械工学の重要な分野に制御工学があります。制御工学では、ある機械を別の機械で制御することができます。例として重量物運搬ロケットを取り上げましょう。ロケットシステムでは、ロケットエンジン、強靭なボディ、そしてコンピューターシステムが連携して飛行を制御します。このように、機械工学と制御工学は一対の車輪のように連動しているといえます。

Lesson 2: Electrical engineering *and* Information engineering

電気工学は電気に関する研究と電気機械の設計を行う学問です。家庭用電気製品はすべて、機能するために電気を使用します。例えば、テレビ、洗濯機、コンピューターはすべて電気を使用します。電気はバッテリー、電源アダプター、その他の電源装置によって機械に供給されます。これらすべての電気製品の電子機能は、電気エンジニアによって設計されています。

情報工学は、コンピューターのハードウェアとソフトウェア、そしてそれらが社会でどのように使われているかを研究する学問です。その良い例がパーソナル・コンピューター（PC）です。パーソナル・コンピューターは、電子メールやワープロのような、私たちがコミュニケーションをとったり文書を作成したりするのに使うソフトウェアを動かします。さらに、コンピューターはインターネットとシームレスに機能するように設計されており、私達は気軽に、音楽を聴いたり、ニュースを読んだり、買い物をしたり、勉強をしたりができ、希望すればソーシャルメディアに参加したりすることもできます。これらのコンピューター機能はすべて、コンピューター・エンジニアによって設計されています。

このハードウェアとソフトウェアがどのように機能するかについては、レッスン3で詳しく説明します。

Lesson 3: The personal computer

個人利用として設計されたコンピューターを、パーソナルコンピューターまたはPCと呼びます。PCにはいくつかの種類があります。まず、標準的なデスクトップコンピューター。次に、より小型でコンパクトなラップトップPCです。日本ではラップトップPCのことをノートブックPCと呼びます。そして、タッチスクリーンを搭載した、タブレットPCです。近年では、タブレットPCの販売台数が増えています。

PCは、多くの部品から構成されています。今日は、CPUあるいは中央演算装置について話します。CPUはコンピュータープログラムを実行する電子回路のことです。例えば、CPUはMicrosoft Word®を使ったり、インターネットのページを閲覧したりするためのコマンドを実行します。CPUは非常に複雑な電子回路です。CPUの性能は、PCの性能に大きく影響します。CPUの処理速度が速いと、PCの処理速度も速くなります。

しかし、高性能なCPUは多くの電力を消費します。したがって、ポータブルPCのバッテリー性能が重要となります。近年では、高い電力密度を有する軽量なリチウムイオンバッテリーが用いられています。

CPUが何をしているか説明できますか？　また、リチウムイオンバッテリーがどうやって電力を貯蔵しているか説明できますか？

Lesson 4: Opto-electronic devices

みなさんはデジタルカメラがどのように機能しているか知っていますか？（＝デジカメの仕組みがわかりますか？）デジカメはダイオードを使用しています。ダイオードはシリコンのような、半導体の材料でできています。今日は、3種類のダイオードについて話をしていきましょう。

最初の種類は、フォトダイオード（（図1）光が当たると電流を発生する半導体素子）です。フォトダイオードは、光を電気信号に変換します。例えば、デジタルカメラのフォトダイオードは、写真画像の光を電気信号に変換します。この信号が画像センサの電気的な入力となります。画像センサは2つの方法で配列することが可能です。一つは、直列センサと呼ばれ、ファックスで使用されます。もう一つは、エリア配列センサと呼ばれています。このタイプは、デジタルカメラ、ビデオカメラ、携帯電話で使用されます。

二つ目のタイプのダイオードは、電気エネルギーを光に変換するものです。これは、発光ダイオード（光を発するダイオード）、またはLEDと呼ばれています（図2）。LEDは交通信号機、電子掲示板などの電気機器で使用されています。みなさんは、LEDを使用している何かほかの機器を思いつきますか。

最後（3つ目）は、レーザーダイオードです。レーザーからの光は非常に強く、集光しています。レーザーダイオードは、CDプレーヤー、レーザープリンターなどの機器に使用されます。

これらすべてのダイオードは「光電変換素子（オプトエレクトロニックデバイス）」と呼ばれています。どうしてかわかりますか？（ヒント：opto＝目の、視力の、光学の、光の）

Lesson 5: Reproduction: Switching of reproductive modes in planarians

生殖は有性生殖と無性生殖に大別されます。「生殖」は似た個体を増やすこと、「性」は遺伝子の混合と定義されます。したがって、有性生殖は、遺伝子の混合を伴った個体の増殖となります。多様性を生み出すことはできますが、生殖コストは高くつきます。無性生殖は遺伝子の混合を伴わず、交尾相手を見つける必要がないため、生殖コストが低くなります。しかしながら、多様性を生み出すことは難しいです。

多くの動物は無性生殖と有性生殖の両方を行います。環境条件に応じて2つの生殖様式を転換させることができます。たとえば、一部の淡水性プラナリアは生殖様式を転換させます（図1）。無性生殖においてプラナリアは体を2分裂させ、その断片が失われた部分を再生します。有性生殖では、雌雄同体性のプラナリアが交尾をして受精卵を含む卵を産みます。

淡水性プラナリア Dugesia japonica （ナミウズムシ）は、夏には無性生殖、冬には有性生殖を行います。季節に応じて2つの生殖様式を使い分けて繁栄してきたと考えられています。

Lesson 6: Ohm's law

この課では、電気回路における基本法則について学習しましょう。それは、オームの法則と呼ばれる法則です。オームの法則は、あらゆる電気回路において用いられます。

図1を見てみましょう。これは基本的な電気回路で、電流を I、電圧を V、抵抗を R で表します。ドイツの物理学者のゲオルク・ジーモン・オーム(1789-1854)は電流が電圧に比例することを発見しました。この発見は今日、「オームの法則」と呼ばれており、以下の式で与えられます。

R は電気抵抗または単に抵抗と呼ばれます。抵抗 R が大きいと電圧 V が一定であれば、電流 I が小さくなります。また同じ条件下（V が一定）では、抵抗 R を小さくすると電流 I が大きくなります。例えば、抵抗が小さい電気回路では、大きな電流を流すことができます。

一方、抵抗 R の逆数をコンダクタンス G と呼びます。コンダクタンス G を用いると、オームの法則は次の式($I=GV$)のように与えられます。例えば、コンダクタンスが大きい場合には、より多くの電流が流れることができます。

では、オームの法則を英語で説明できますか？まず、電流、電圧、抵抗そしてコンダクタンスの説明が必要なことに留意しましょう。

Lesson 7: Solar power generation with photovoltaic (PV) cells

　「再生可能エネルギー」は、化石燃料や原子力以外の資源での発電を表すために使われる用語です。今日は、太陽電池を用いて発電する方法に注目します。これは、「太陽光発電」と呼ばれています。

　太陽電池（PV セル）は、太陽光を電気エネルギーに変換します。そのために、結晶シリコンなどの半導体材料が使われています（図1）。この図について説明できますか？

　PV モジュールは、複数の PV セルから構成されています。PV モジュールには2種類あります。一つ目は集光式と呼ばれるものです。集光式モジュール（図2）は、レンズを使って太陽光を PV セルに集光します。しかし、焦点を合わせるためには太陽を正確に追尾する必要があります。そのため、コストと複雑さが増えます。二つ目のタイプは、平板モジュール（図3）と呼ばれるもので、一定の角度で設置されます。これは、太陽光発電所でよく使われています。

　PV モジュールが発電する直流（DC）電力を直接、一般家庭で使用したり電力系統に送電したりすることができません。そのため、直流電力を交流（AC）電力に変換する必要があります。

　太陽光発電の普及は、エネルギー分野における二酸化炭素の排出量の削減だけでなく、国家のエネルギーの安全保障を強化するうえでも極めて重要です。今後、太陽光発電は我々の社会でより重要な役割を果たすことが期待されています。

Lesson 8: Genome editing: A mouse with GFP

　近年、ゲノムを基盤としたバイオテクノロジーが急速に発展しています。「ゲノム」とは生物の全遺伝情報のことです。それぞれの種は、その種特異的なゲノムを持っています。ゲノムの主な分子はデオキシリボ核酸です（DNA）。全ての生物において、DNA は親から子へ受け継がれています。

　タンパク質は全ての生命現象において最も重要な分子です。「遺伝子」と呼ばれる DNA 配列がタンパク質の設計図として働いています。これは、遺伝子がタンパク質を合成するための資源であることを意味しています。例えば、クラゲのゲノムには緑色蛍光タンパク質（GFP）を合成するための遺伝子が存在しています。GFP は紫外線を吸収した時に緑色蛍光を発します。

　今日、GFP は多くの生命科学で利用されています。例えば、マウスのタンパク質と GFP の「融合タンパク質」を作ることができます。そのために、クラゲに由来する GFP 遺伝子がマウスゲノムの正確な場所に置かれます（組み替えられます）。図1を見てみましょう。この図を説明できますか。この方法が完了すると、培養系のマウスの生細胞で緑色の蛍光を見たり、生体内で細胞のふるまいをたどったりできます。

　この方法は CRISPR/Cas9 と呼ばれる「ゲノム改変技術」です。CRISPR/Cas9 は素早く、正確に、低価格でゲノム改変することを可能にしました。

　最近では、CRISPR/Cas9 を使ったゲノム改変が様々な種を使った研究プロジェクトで利用されています。ゲノム改変は重要な技術的進歩です。しかし、危険性もあります。例えば、ヒトの胚に CRISPR/Cas9 が使用された例が報告されました。これは明らかに、このバイオテクノロジーの倫理上の危険性を示しています。我々は、技術的な革新は潜在的に諸刃の剣であることを決して忘れてはいけないのです。

Lesson 9: Mechatronics I

　「メカトロニクス」は和製英語です。この言葉は、運動機能と制御機能が一体化しているシステムのことを指します。例えば、図1を見てください。これは、両腕がコンピューターによって制御された電気モーターによって動くロボットです。

　メカトロニクスロボットはさまざまな産業で使われています。例えば、トヨタのような自動車メーカーは、自動車を製造するための工場でロボットを使用します。エンジンのような重い部品を車の中に移動させるものもあれば、溶接をするものもあります。他にも、メカトロニクスやロボットができるかもしれないことを思いつきますか。

　では、メカトロニクスロボットについてもっと詳しく見ていきましょう。まず、このロボットはプログラム可能な機能を備えています。つまり、コンピューターをプログラムして何かをさせることができます。マイクロコンピューター（表1参照）がそのプログラムを実行します。これによって機械のアクチュエーター

が作動します。次に機械はその作業を確認することができます。そのためにセンサーを使用します。例えば、図1のカメラは機械が書いたものを確認しています。書かれた文字は正しいですか？　もし正しくなければ、機械が停止するか、人間に問題があることを知らせます。

　図1のロボットは何と書いているでしょうか。どうやってそれをやっているのでしょうか。（ヒント：「マイクロコンピュータ」から始めてみましょう。）

Lesson 10: Using Ohm's law and Kirchhoff's laws

　オームの法則とキルヒホッフの法則は、工学の講義で学習済みです。ここでは、それらの法則を使って電気回路の計算を行いましょう。
・オームの法則の利用
（1）図1において、抵抗 R に流れ込む電流の大きさはいくらか？
（2）図2において、1.5 V の電源がランプに接続されている。この時、電流は 0.3 A であった。抵抗とランプのコンダクタンスの値はいくらか？
・キルヒホッフの法則の利用
（3）図3において、それぞれの抵抗に流れ込む電流の大きさはいくらか？

＜解答＞以下の数式を英語で音読できますか？

Lesson 11: F1 aerodynamics

　F1は「Formula One」の略称です。フォーミュラー・ワンは自動車レースの最高峰カテゴリです。F1マシンの速度、加速度さらに安定性の向上に、機械工学と制御工学が非常に重要な役割を果たします。それは、どのようなものでしょうか？

　では、空気力学に着目してみましょう。空気力学は、物体（例えば車両や航空機）周辺の空気の流れについて研究する分野です。空気力学の目的は、抗力（抗力：進行方向の反対の方向に作用する力）を減少させることです。図1を見てみましょう。これは、翼まわりの空気の流れを表しています。抗力を低減することは、航空機や車両の性能を向上させます。トヨタのプリウスやホンダのインサイトは優れた空力設計の例です。

　（フォーミュラーカーと一般車両とでは）競技車両の方が抗力が小さいと思いませんか？　答えは「NO」です。フォーミュラーカーでは、空気力学は抗力ではなくダウンフォースを増加させるために用いられます。ダウンフォースは、車両を地面に押し付ける力です。フォーミュラーカーは、大きな推進力を得てコーナーを高速で走行するために、タイヤと地面との間に大きな摩擦力を必要とします。ダウンフォースはその摩擦力を増加させ、フォーミュラーカーを安定させます。

　フォーミュラーカーのその大きなダウンフォースは、理論的には、フォーミュラーカーがトンネルの天井を走行できるほどです。みなさんは抗力とダウンフォースの違いが説明できますか？

Lesson 12: Applied chemistry: Creating instant ramen through sublimation

　化学は物質について研究・探求する学問である。この単元では、化学の力を利用してインスタントラーメンやインスタントコーヒーのような「フリーズドライ」食品をつくることに注目します。これらの製品はスーパーマーケットで陳列されていても傷むことがなく大変便利です。

　知っての通り、我々の身の回りに存在する物質は固体、液体、もしくは気体状態にあります。ラーメンをフリーズドライするために、ラーメンから液体の水を安全かつ衛生的に除く必要があります。これは真空化で食品を凍らせることで実行できます。これにより水は液体を経由せず固体から気体へ状態変化します。この現象は「昇華」と呼ばれます。

　これはどんな仕組みになっているでしょうか？　物質の状態は温度と圧力に依存しています。物質の温度・圧力と、状態の関係をまとめた図は状態図と呼ばれます。図1に水の状態図を示します。

　水の温度と圧力条件を、図1に示された経路に沿って変化させることを考えてみましょう。まず、水は点 X に示される条件（1気圧、室温）では液体として存在しています。矢印1に示すように、圧力を一定に保

ったままで温度を減少させると、点Yで示される条件となります。次に、矢印2で示すように温度を一定に保ったままで、圧力を低下させます。驚くことに、固体の水は液体を経由せず直接気体へ変化、すなわち昇華します。

図1を説明できますか？　これがインスタントラーメンや他の多くの製品を支えている技術です。この技術を理解しましたか？　昇華が何かを説明できますか？

Lesson 13: Mechatronics II

工学系の学生は国内や国際的なロボットのコンテスト（ロボコン）に参加することができます。コンテストには様々な種類があります。今日は、泳ぐロボットのコンテストについて話をしていきましょう。具体的には、ウミガメロボットに注目します。

亀のロボットを作るためには、私たちはまず、亀がどうやって泳ぐかを理解しなければなりません。簡単な泳ぐ亀の運動模型を作るために、画像データ処理技術を使って情報を収集します。

次に、亀が泳ぐ様子を模倣する技術をどうやって作り出すことができるかを検討します。写真1と2を見てください。これは、PICマイクロコンピューターを使ってCDサーボモーターをコントロールする研究モデルです。このモーターは翼の形をした足ひれ（フィン）を動かします。フィンは速く振ったりゆっくり振ったりすることができ、これは、亀を前に動かすための強い揚力を作り出すことができます。

揚力は速度の二乗に比例するので、フィンを上下に振る速度と足ひれの角度は泳ぎの安定と速さに対して重要なパラメーターとなります。さらに、マイクロコンピューターが正確にモーターを制御できるように、スピードや、位置、圧力を計測するセンサーの位置がとても重要になります。

これらの研究モデルは水中のロボットコンテストでの競技用に開発されています。多くの場合、私たちが初めてロボットを作ると、その動きは多少ぎこちないものになります。したがって、手足の動き、センサーからのフィードバック、ロボットの形状などを改善しなければなりません。したがって、ロボコンで勝つためにはチームワークが非常に重要になります。ロボコンチームに加わって、競争に参加してみたいですか？

Lesson 14: Information literacy

情報リテラシーとは、あなたが必要な情報を特定し、最適な情報源を見つけ、それらの情報源を批判的に評価し、情報を共有できる能力のことです。例えば、エンジン設計について情報が必要であれば、専門的なレポートや雑誌、そのほかの情報源を検索する能力が必要です。そうすることで、知識の基盤が成長します。技術や社会に関する現在の問題を理解できるようになり、学校や職場で効果的に協力しあえるようになります。

私たちは、増大し続ける情報のネットワークに囲まれているため、情報リテラシーは非常に重要です。しかしながら、問題がある場合もあります。すべての情報が公平に生み出されているわけではなく、最新で信頼できる情報もあれば、偏った情報、時代遅れの情報、誤解を招く情報、あるいは単なる虚偽の情報もあります。

さらに、セキュリティの問題もあります。ネットワークにつながったコンピューターは常にウィルスの脅威にさらされています。たとえパスワードで保護されているとしても、あなたのコンピューターはネットワークを通じて攻撃される可能性があります。例えば、ウィルス感染はOSのセキュリティホールをかいくぐって起こりえます。また、ウィルスは電子メールの添付ファイルやダウンロードしたフリーソフトを通じてコンピューターに感染する可能性もあります。一度ウィルスに感染したコンピューターは、他のコンピューターへとウィルスを拡散し、何千通ものスパムメールを送りつけるかもしれません。したがって、セキュリティ技術について知ることは情報リテラシーの中で重要な側面です。

結論として、わたしたちは情報リテラシーを身につける必要があり、そうすることで情報や研究の世界に参加可能となり、同時にセキュリティ問題も理解できるようになります。

Lesson 15: When "information recommendation" meets AI

インターネット上でショッピングする際、そのウェブサイトは、頻繁にあなたへのオススメ商品を紹介します。例えば、本や新しいコンピューターゲームを「オススメ」されることがあります。あなたはこれを便利だと思いますか？　これは「情報推薦」と呼ばれ、多くの人が便利だと考えています。

1998年、アマゾンはユーザーに対して、類似する商品を推薦する初めてのサービスを公開しました。このサービスは「協調フィルタリング」（CF）と呼ばれる簡単な行列計算のアルゴリズムに基づいて開発されました。Fig. 1 を見てください。CF がどのように機能するか理解できますか？　現在、ユーザーに閲覧されたアマゾンウェブページの約 30％は「オススメ」によるものと報告されています。

現在、情報推薦は「ビッグデータ」と人工知能(AI)のブームよりかなり強化されています。推薦システムは蓄積された膨大なデータと大規模並列処理の両方を取り入れて、ユーザーのプロフィールを構築しています。システムはユーザーの履歴レーティングのみならず、文書や写真画像も利用しています。つまり、CFの代わりに人工知能技術の一種である機械学習が用いられています。システムは数学モデルを確立し、時間や季節、さらにユーザーの商品を購入する順序といったユーザーの購買習慣パターンを認識します。これにより、従来の CF よりも正確なオススメを提供することができます。

つまり、新しい推薦システムはあなた自身よりも、あなたのことを理解しているかもしれないのです。CF と AI に基づいた推薦システムがどのように機能するのかを説明することができますか？

Lesson 16: Space junk: The problem of waste in space

注意）本文では、junk と debris はどちらも同じような意味で使われています。junk は「ガラクタ、ゴミ」、debris は「壊れたもの、破壊されたものの破片」という意味です。この和訳では junk ＝ ゴミ、debris ＝デブリで統一しています。

皆さんも知っているように、地球上には大量のごみの問題があります。しかし、宇宙にも大量のごみの問題があることを知っていましたか？　多くの古い人工衛星や古い宇宙機器が地球の軌道を回っています。これらのごみは不要なものです。これらは「宇宙デブリ」または、単に「宇宙ゴミ」と呼ばれています。今日は、どうしてこの宇宙ゴミが大きな問題であるかについて話をしましょう。

最初の問題：宇宙ゴミはとても速いスピードで移動しています。典型的な宇宙ゴミは秒速 7-8 キロメートルの速さで移動しています。したがって、衝突時の相対的な速度は秒速 10 キロメートルに達する場合があります。この速度について考えてみましょう。速い車は 1 秒間にどれくらい移動できるだろうか？　ジェット機は（1 秒間にどれぐらい移動できる）？　秒速 7-8 キロメートルの想像ができますか？　もしこの宇宙ゴミがほかの宇宙船にぶつかったとしたら、たとえ、それがとても小さかったとしても、その宇宙船を損傷または破壊してしまうでしょう。知っているように、運動エネルギーは以下の方程式に示されているように、速度の二乗に比例します。

2 番目の問題：古い人工衛星が壊れると、多くの小さい部品（デブリ）は、また高速で移動するし宇宙に拡散します。これらの小さい部品は何度も何度も分裂し、最終的に、図に示すように、デブリ雲を形成します。

今日では、直径 10 センチメートル以上のデブリは、衝突を避けるために、NASA や JAXA といった機関で監視されています。NASA はどうやってこれらすべてのゴミを追跡していると思いますか？　難しいですね。この問題やほかの宇宙の問題については、後のレッスンで話し合うことにしましょう。今は、宇宙デブリについて学んだことを復習してください。

[問題]　微小な宇宙デブリの運動エネルギーを計算してみましょう。（質量 M=1 kg、　速度 V=10 km/s）

Lesson 17: Air pollution and control technology

大気汚染は、今日私たちが直面している深刻な環境問題であり、その原因は私たち人間の活動です。大気汚染にはさまざまな種類があります。たとえば、ガソリン車から（排出される）一酸化炭素やゴミの焼却から生じるダイオキシンです。さらに、石炭や液化天然ガス(LNG)を燃やして発電することで、私たちは大量の二酸化炭素を排出しています。そして、それは地球の温暖化を引き起こしています。

日本には多くの工場がありそれらの工場は、1960 年代、70 年代に深刻な環境破壊を引き起こしました。

今日（こんにち）、日本においては地球環境にやさしい技術開発や、市民による個々の努力により深刻な大気汚染の量は減少しています。一方で、大気汚染は未だにアジア、特に、高度経済成長している地域や、人口爆発（急激な増加）がある地域において深刻な問題です。多くの場合、これら地域の工場や自動車による大気汚染は、効果的に規制されていません。

　表1を見てください。この表は、工場のある都市部において最もひどい汚染物質をいくつか示しています。これら汚染物質はいまなお日本や世界中で排出されており、私達はすべての汚染物質を減らすための努力を続ける必要があります。

　大気に放たれた二酸化炭素の量を減らすことは、今日最も大きな難題（挑戦）の一つです。大気汚染や地球温暖化を含む多くの環境問題を改善するために、皆さん方が学んでいる科学技術は非常に重要です。

Lesson 18: Airbus vs. Boeing

　かつて、航空機市場においては、大型機が主流であったが、近年は、A320neo や B737MAX のような小型機の人気が高まっている。この理由には、多頻度運航への乗客の需要の高まりだけではなく、燃料費の削減と CO_2 排出量削減の要求がある。その結果、大型の B747-8 と A380 型機の受注数は 0 に落ち込んだ。一方で、小型機への需要は増加を続けており、かくして、小型機の受注は、2022 会計年度のエアバスの総受注 1,078 機の94%を占めた。ボーイングにおいても、状況は同じで、2022 会計年度の総受注 774 機の72%を占めている。

　エアバスとボーイングの小型機戦略の違いを見ていこう。

エアバスは、1980 年代末期に初飛行した A320 シリーズを基に、現在は A320neo(標準座席数 150-180 席)と A321neo(標準座席数 180-220)ファミリーを提供している。これらの航空機は、効率性と燃料消費の継続的な改善が行われている。小型機といえば、一般的に短距離路線をイメージさせるが、A321XLR(エキストラ・ロング・レンジ)は、4,700 海里(約 8,700km)の航続距離をもつ。これは、A321XLR が、東京からアメリカ西海岸、オーストラリア、東欧までノンストップで飛行できることを意味する。

　一方、737MAX ファミリーで、ボーイングはエアバスに対抗する。737 シリーズは、1967 年の初飛行以来、世界で最も売れている飛行機である。737 シリーズの標準座席数は 138-230 席であり、航続距離は最長で 3,825 海里(約 7,084km)である。この飛行機は、半世紀以上にもわたって運用されているので、航空会社やパイロットの信頼を獲得しており、また、設計とエンジンの改良により、継続的に効率化を図っている。さらに、コックピットレイアウトは、どんどん進化し、ボーイングの最新機種である 787 シリーズのものに類似するグラスコックピットを取り入れ、パイロットの作業量を軽減している。

　2022 年 12 月にユナイテッド航空は、100 機の 737MAX ファミリーを発注し、また、2023 年 2 月には、エアインディアも 210 機の A320 ファミリーを発注するなど、小型機への世界的な需要は、とどまるところを知らない勢いで増加している。したがって、ANA やユナイテッド航空などの航空会社は、A320neo や B737MAX のような飛行機のうち、どちらかを選ばなければならない。どのような要因(この文章で議論された)が意思決定の動機となっているとあなたは考えるか？

Answers to the exercises

Lesson 1

Discussion:	(Find the answers in the text, or write your opinions.)
Exercises:	A. (Find the answers in the text.) B. (Find the answers in the text.) C. (adj) biological, (n) development, a development
Translation:	Note: the translations below are examples. Other versions are possible. 1. Science and engineering are fields of study related to each other. / Science and engineering are interrelated related fields of study. 2. Precise measurements are important in both science and engineering. 3. My car is one of the latest models, and is designed to be very friendly to the environment. 4. My teacher often uses rocket engines as an example to explain external combustion engines.
Writing (sample Summary)	This text is about Advanced science and Mechanical engineering. It starts with Advanced science. It says that there were only a few branches of engineering in the past. However, recently new branches have started, like genetic engineering. Because of this, skills in Advanced science have become more important. I think this is great. I really like the new disciplines and I want to become an expert in laboratory techniques. Next it talks about Mechanical engineering. It uses the examples of cars and rockets. I think this is fantastic. I want to work in car design and make exciting new cars.

Lesson 2

Exercises:	C. (n) electricity (adj) electronic / electric (n) a supply, (v) to equip
Translation:	1. We study electrical engineering to become engineers. 2. I want to master English to work abroad. 3. The Internet became a part of our lives. 4. What has information engineering brought to our lives?

Lesson 3

Exercises:	C. (adv) individually, (n) programming (v) to program
Translation:	1. Last month, the company released some new computers. 2. One of them is a lap-top type, and it is designed so that beginners can use it. 3. It is made with minimum parts but has sufficient capabilities to create reports and send e-mails. 4. It is the lightest and cheapest of all the company's computers.

Lesson 4

Exercises:	C. (n) an arrangement, (n) an emission, emissions, (v) to print
Translation:	1. There are two types of electrical current. One is called Direct Current (DC). The other is called Alternating Current (AC). 2. AC is used for electrical appliances at home. 3. This adaptor converts AC to DC. 4. Recent traffic lights use LEDs, and incandescent light bulbs are being replaced.

Lesson 5

Exercises:	C. (v) to reproduce, (v) to diversify, (n) fertility / fertilization
Translation:	1. Many animals can reproduce both asexually and sexually. 2. Asexual reproduction cannot produce diversity. 3. There is also a group of freshwater planarians that do not change their mode of reproduction. 4. Freshwater planarians change from asexual reproduction to sexual reproduction between summer and winter.

Lesson 6

Exercises:	C. (adv) basically, (n) physics, (n) a discovery
Translation:	1. Ohm's Law is fundamental knowledge in electrical engineering. 2. The current running in this electrical circuit was calculated using Ohm's law. 3. Rare metals are used to imrove the capabilities of electric appliances. 4. On the other hand, many rare metals are unconsciously dumped.

Lesson 7

Exercises:	C. (v) to renew, (n) a description, (adj) accurate, (adj) complex, (adj) secure
Translation:	1. Photovoltaic (PV) solar power generation does not use fossil fuels when producing electricity. 2. Concentrator modules are composed of solar cells, lenses, and solar tracking devices. 3. One reason the amount of PV solar power generation has increased is the reduction of costs. 4. The introduction of PV energy generation is an effective way to prevent global warming.

Lesson 8

Exercises:	C. (v) to sequence, (n) a synthesis, (v) to innovate, (v) to modify
Translation:	1. Because genomes vary by species, one could say that species diversity is genome diversity. 2. Dr. Osamu Shimomura won the Nobel Prize for discovering and isolating the Green Fluorescent Protein in the genome of a jellyfish. 3. CRSPR of CRSPR/Cas9 are repeated sequences in the genomes of bacteria, and were discovered by Japanese researchers in 1987. 4. It is not uncommon for knowledge gained from basic research to be applied by other researchers and lead to technological innovation.

Lesson 9

Exercises:	C. (n) a reference, (adj) industrial, (v) to industrialize, (n) manufacturing, (v) to manufacture
Translation:	1. Let's look at the manual in detail before consulting with the support desk. / Let's read the manual carefully before consulting the support desk. 2. The manual shows us how to use the machine and troubleshooting. 3. We make the machine draw straight lines and curved lines. 4. If there is a problem, we can have the machine fixed by the vendor.

Lesson 10

Exercises:	C. (n) an analysis, (v) to conduct, (v) to equate
Translation:	1. We learned how to draw an electrical diagram. 2. According to the diagram, the storage batteries are connected to two lights. 3. What is the value of the current? 4. Use a formula to calculate the circuit's voltage and current.

Lesson 11

Exercises:	C. (adj) aerodynamic, (n) an increase, (n) a decrease
Translation:	1. Cars play an important role these days. 2. Cars make our daily lives convenient. 3. What's important is making safe cars. 4. Engineers research day by day to improve both the safety performance and environmental performance of cars.

Lesson 12

Exercises:	C. (v) to sublimate, (v) to sanitize, (v) to pressurize
Translation:	1. The results of this experiment show that the target molecule is being generated. / Experient results suggest the target molecule is being generated. 2. Chart 1 shows the measurement results. 3. I surveyed the relationship between temperature and pressure. / The relationship between temperature and pressure was investigated. 4. I changed the temperature and performed an experiment. / Experiments were conducted by varying the temperature.

Lesson 13

Exercises:	C. (n) participation, (n) stability, (v) to stabilize, (n) precision, (adv) precisely
Translation:	1. My dream is to go to university and participate in the robot contest for university students. 2. So, I am studying very hard now to be able to enter university. 3. I am also gaining expertise by studying subjects related to robotics. 4. Do you want to learn mechatronics too?

Lesson 14

Exercises:	C. (n) an evaluation, (n) reliability, (v) to infect
Translation:	1. He receives hundreds of e-mails every day. 2. Actually, he doesn't read every e-mail. 3. He is afraid that his computer might become infected with a virus, so he sometimes doesn't open some e-mails. 4. As a result, he sometimes misses important information and trouble is caused at work.

Lesson 15

Exercises:	C. (n) an enhancement, (v) to accumulate, (n) recognition
Translation:	1. Both collaborative filtering and machine learning methods are based on user data. 2. User profiles are used as big data, and systems make accurate predictions. 3. If you are not sure where to go on vacation, it is a good idea to use a sightseeing recommendation system. 4. People who bought this product also bought these products.

Lesson 16

Exercises:	C. (adv) typically, (n) destruction, (v) to collide
Translation:	1. What I am learning right now is related to robotics. 2. Even if it is difficult, I intend to become a robotics engineer. 3. I review the textbook over and over again as the teacher says. 4. How do you think I can get a good grade on the next test?

Lesson 17

Exercises:	C. (v) to grow, (n) an improvement, (v) to chlorinate
Translation:	1. We are currently facing many environmental problems. 2. We use large amounts of plastic every day. 3. The plastic we use is creating a trash problem. 4. Reducing the amount of trash is important for the earth's environment.

Lesson 18

Exercises:	C. (adj) strategic, (v) to operate, (n) motivation
Translation:	1. Airplanes made by Boeing account for 60% of the world's commercial aircraft. 2. The capacity of this car is 8 persons. 3. Automated driving technology reduces the workload of drivers. 4. The demand for efficiency in products is unstoppable.

Vocabulary Index

( ) = Lesson

equation (6, 10)
equipment   (2)
to establish   (15)
ethical   (8)
to
evaluate   (14)
evaluation   (14)
to evolve   (18)
to execute   (3)
to expose   (14)

F
to face   (17)
factor   (18)
feedback   (13)
fertilization   (5)
to fertilize   (5)
field   (1)
to filter   (15)
fin   (13)
flight   (1)
flow   (11)
to flow   (10)
fluorescent   (8)
to focus   (4, 7)
force   (13)
fragment   (5)
freeze-dried   (12)
freshwater   (5)
frequently   (15)
friction   (11)
fuel   (7)
to function   (2)
function   (2, 9)
fundamental   (6)
furthermore (2)
fusion   (8)

G
gaseous   (12)
gene   (5, 8)
genetic   (1)
genome   (8)
goal   (11)
goods   (2)

grid   (7)
to grow   (17)
growth   (17)

H
hardware   (2)
hazardous   (17)
household   (2)
however   (3)

I
to identify   (14)
image   (4)
impact   (16)
to improve   (17)
improvement   (17)
increase   (11)
to increase   (11)
to indicate   (12)
individual   (3, 5)
individually   (3)
industrial   (9)
to industrialize   (9)
industry   (9)
to infect   (14)
infection   (14)
to inherit   (8)
interdisciplinary   (1)
ion   (3)
to innovate   (8)
innovation   (8)
input   (4)
instructions   (9)
to involve   (5)
irradiance   (7)

J
journal   (14)
to judge   (9)
junk   (16)

K
kinetic   (16)
knee   (13)
knowledge   (14)

L
lap   (3)
laser   (4)
to launch   (15)
law   (6)
to lay   (5)
lift   (13)
limb   (9)
linear   (4)
literacy   (14)
lithium   (3)
location   (13)

M
machine   (1)
mainstream   (18)
to maintain   (7)
to manufacture   (9)
manufacturer   (9)
manufacturing   (9)
mate   (5)
to mate   (5)
material   (1, 4)
mathematical   (15)
matter   (12)
maximum   (18)
measurement   (1)
mechanical   (1)
to mimic   (13)
mode   (5)
model   (13)
modification   (8)
module   (7)
molecule   (8)
to monitor   (16)
monoxide   (17)
moreover   (17)
motion   (13)
to motivate   (18)
motivation   (18)
motor   (9)
to mount   (7)
movement   (11)

therefore (16)

threat (14)

thrust (11)

thus (5)

tough (1)

to track (7, 16)

traffic (4)

transmission (1)

to travel (16)

tunnel (11)

type (3)

typical (16)

typically (16)

U

ultraviolet (8)

useless (16)

V

vacuum (12)

value (6, 10)

various (17)

to vary (12)

vehicle (16)

velocity (16)

voltage (6)

W

wall (11)

washing machine (2)

waste (16)

welding (9)

widespread (7)

word processor (2)

workload (18)

──編 著 者 紹 介──

津山工業高等専門学校　技術英語テキスト改訂ワーキンググループ

代表者：　Eric Rambo　（教授：情報システム系）
副代表者：加藤　学　（教授：機械システム系）
執筆者：　Eric Rambo　（教授：情報システム系）
　　　　　寺元貴幸　（教授：情報システム系）
　　　　　柴田典人　（教授：先進科学系）
　　　　　細谷和範　（教授：機械システム系）
　　　　　加藤　学　（教授：機械システム系）
　　　　　西尾公裕　（教授：電気電子システム系）
　　　　　桶　真一郎　（教授：電気電子システム系）
　　　　　山田貴史　（准教授：機械システム系）
　　　　　前澤孝信　（准教授：先進科学系）
　　　　　島田悠彦　（准教授：先進科学系）
　　　　　房　冠深　（准教授：情報システム系）
　　　　　守友博紀　（講師：先進科学系）
　　　　　Patrick Palmer　（助手：先進科学系）

Ⓒ津山工業高等専門学校　技術英語テキスト改訂ワーキンググループ 2024

改訂新版　技術英語 実践的技術英語テキスト 初級〜中級レベル

2010年 3月31日　　　第1版第1刷発行
2024年 2月 9日　改訂第1版第1刷発行

　　　　　　津 山 工 業 高 等 専 門 学 校
編　　者　技 術 英 語 テ キ ス ト 改 訂
　　　　　ワ ー キ ン グ グ ル ー プ
発 行 者　田　　　中　　　聡

発 行 所
株式会社 電 気 書 院
ホームページ　www.denkishoin.co.jp
（振替口座　00190-5-18837）
〒101-0051　東京都千代田区神田神保町 1-3 ミヤタビル 2F
電話(03)5259-9160／FAX(03)5259-9162

印刷　創栄図書印刷株式会社
Ⓒ Cover photo：K.Hosotani "Swimming Robot"
Printed in Japan／ISBN978-4-485-30123-4